Cambridge Studies in Social Anthropology

General Editor: Jack Goody

37

THE ANTHROPOLOGICAL CIRCLE

This book is published as part of the joint publishing agreement established in 1977 between the Fondation de la Maison des Sciences de l'Homme and the Press Syndicate of the University of Cambridge. Titles published under this arrangement may appear in any European language, or, in the case of volumes of collected essays, in several languages.

New books will appear either as individual titles or in one of the series which the Maison des Sciences de l'Homme and the Cambridge University Press have jointly agreed to publish. All books published jointly by the Maison des Sciences de l'Homme and the Cambridge University Press will be distributed by the Press throughout the world.

Cet ouvrage est publié dans le cadre de l'accord de co-édition passé en 1977 entre la Fondation de la Maison des Sciences de l'Homme et le Press Syndicate of the University of Cambridge. Toutes les langues européennes sont admises pour les titres couverts par cet accord, et les ouvrages collectifs peuvent paraître en plusieurs langues.

Les ouvrages paraissent soit isolément, soit dans l'une des séries que la Maison des Sciences de l'Homme et Cambridge University Press ont convenu de publier ensemble. La distribution dans le monde entier des titres ainsi publiés conjointement par les deux établissements est assurée par Cambridge University Press.

The Anthropological Circle

Symbol, Function, History

MARC AUGÉ

Directeur d'Etudes, Ecole des Hautes
Etudes en Sciences Sociales, Paris

Translated by MARTIN THOM

CAMBRIDGE UNIVERSITY PRESS

Cambridge
London   New York   New Rochelle   Melbourne   Sydney

and

EDITIONS DE LA MAISON DES SCIENCES DE L'HOMME
Paris

Published by the Press Syndicate of the University of Cambridge
The Pitt Building, Trumpington Street, Cambridge CB2 1RP
32 East 57th Street, New York, NY 10022, USA
296 Beaconsfield Parade, Middle Park, Melbourne 3206, Australia
and Editions de la Maison des Sciences de l'Homme
54 Boulevard Raspail, 75270 Paris Cedex 06

Originally published in French as *Symbole, Fonction, Histoire* by Hachette,
Paris, 1979. © Hachette 1979

First published in English by Editions de la Maison des Sciences de l'Homme
and Cambridge University Press 1982 as *The Anthropological Circle*
English translations © Maison des Sciences de l'Homme
and Cambridge University Press 1982

Printed in Great Britain by
Western Printing Services Ltd, Bristol

Library of Congress catalogue card number: 81–7647

British Library Cataloguing in Publication Data

Augé, Marc
The anthropological circle. – (Cambridge studies in social anthropology)
1. Ethnology
I. Title   II. Symbole, fonction, histoire. *English*
306   GN316

ISBN 0 521 23236 8 hard covers
ISBN 0 521 28548 8 paperback

Contents

Preface   vii

**Introduction. Anthropology without history or
   anthropology in history?**   1

1. The anthropological circle   14
Two axes and four poles   14
Evolution, culture, symbol   18
Evolution, culture, function   22
Symbol, function   25
Symbol, function, culture   33
Culture, symbol   36

2. Some questions concerning the current state of anthropology   42
The philosopher's questions   42
Meaning, non-meaning and structure: Claude Lévi-Strauss   50
Symbol and function: Victor Turner   61
Instances and determination: Marxist anthropology   65

3. From moral crisis to intellectual doubt   78
The object of anthropology   79
Ethnocentrism and anti-ethnocentrism   90
Scientific practice, militant practice   94

Conclusions   101
New sites, new stakes   101
Here, today   102

Contents

Social logics   108
A myth, a necessity: interdisciplinarity   111

Notes   116

Index   125

Preface

The reader will perhaps be surprised to find that, in my treatment of current anthropological perspectives, I have devoted the best part of this book to French authors and theoretical tendencies. I have chosen to speak of research in progress, of new and tentative approaches and of realignments that in some cases have hardly assumed a definite shape at all. For, while I have no intention of repudiating the official canon, I take it that these new approaches do supersede it and that they delineate a possible future for a critical analysis of the logic of social institutions. In this respect my knowledge of recent or half-completed work, of provocative intellectual currents and theoretical developments abroad, cannot help but be less profound and less in touch, hence my focus on French research. This admission does not, however, render the above hypothesis null and void. For I would maintain that French anthropology, in spite or because of its sometimes excessive taste for theoretical debate (which makes it both receptive to philosophical discussion and vulnerable to intellectual fashions), is at present assembling the basic elements for a novel reflection on the necessary conditions for, and meaning of, a synthetic science, both anthropological and historical, of men in society. I would also argue that this debate, conducted in terms of structuralism and Marxism, is far more advanced in France than in countries with an Anglo-Saxon anthropological tradition.

Finally, let me stress that this work would not make much sense if it were nothing more than a catalogue; it therefore includes elements of assessment. I do not claim, however, in the name of some revealed truth, to award good or bad marks, but rather to take up *positions* in relation to other formulations.

Introduction. Anthropology without history or anthropology in history?

This work is not situated in the same conceptual space as the several excellent histories of anthropology[1] currently available in France. In that they testify to the uncertainties and questionings of a discipline whose first problem is that of defining itself, these histories comprise the field of analysis and reflection of this work. It is something of a paradox that a discipline that has a fair number of researchers still hesitates over which name to choose (anthropology or ethnology) and over the nature of its boundaries (most obviously, those that separate history from sociology). In so far as this is something more than a verbal quibble or confrontation within the universities, and given the empire-building activities that take place there, this hesitation is all the more serious, and bears quite centrally on the meaning and object of our research. What have we sought (if not found)? What are we looking for?

We therefore have to take stock; not because the materials we have accumulated are so significant that we ought to try to evaluate and classify them, but rather because the sheer range of different trajectories and approaches, and consequent confusion of paths, obliges us to attempt a clarification. If an itinerary has been discovered, or rather created and constituted, what is it and where are we going wrong? The problem with anthropologists is not so much one of knowing if they do or do not agree, but more one of understanding if they are speaking of the same thing or not.

The almost paradoxical maturity that anthropology has achieved makes this question all the more urgent, since, as a consequence of this maturity, its prestige, or at any rate, its influence, has grown in direct ratio to its own profound disarray and internal divisions. Several factors may be adduced to account for the attraction that anthropology, albeit in haphazard or misleading forms, now holds for a fairly wide public. There is, first of all, the day-to-day impact of bureaucratic constraints. These are not exactly successful in making individuals believe, given the manner in which their time is taken up with compulsory activities, that when they consume, they are essentially consuming freely, and such constraints therefore arouse or revive

1

that taste for other times and other places that has so often characterised the sensibility of westerners. It is an old tradition, certainly, and an artfully ethnocentric one, stirring up a nostalgia, a desire for escape and a need for comparison in the depths of narcissistic reflection in which European intellectuals indulge. The Middle Ages were never finer than under romanticism and savages were never more attractive than in the eighteenth century. Montaigne himself had been captivated by the Amerindians' wisdom and had, like Rousseau and Montesquieu after him, used it as a pretext for reflecting critically on European customs and institutions. He thus established a sensibility and a form of thought that still affect us residually, as much in the writings of the romantics as in the aesthetic and political agitations of the surrealists, and in the most sophisticated of monographs also.

But there is something else at stake now, as both this desire for 'the other' and this self-torment have become more extreme, more crude yet more subtle. Now the intellectuals' notion of luxury would seem to be identified with the dissatisfaction of the common run of mortals. 'The distant coconut palms of proud Africa' haunted the Paris of both Baudelaire and Mallarmé, as did invitations to depart, whether for life or for death; but until recently this was only for those who had had the privilege of further education and, as readers of Castex and Surer and Lagarde and Michard, had fed listlessly off these images. Today, the invitation is extended more widely; travel agents offer us a wide range of brightly coloured illustrations that demand our attention and sometimes, because of a chance tiredness or desire, or because of a lucky camera angle, actually move us.

For the European 'consumer' the world does not become less exotic as it grows more familiar. In dreaming of a cruise to North Africa, if his demands are modest, or if you like, to black Africa, the European will hardly pay any attention to those who come from there. The day-to-day proximity of migrant workers beside our dustbins, drains and building-sites gives them an almost abstract character, and one that is in curious contrast to the concrete urgency of dreams of escape. The discovery of another humanity can hardly be said to be the true concern of the numerous enthusiasts of charter flights, round trips, and holidays in which one undertakes 'exploration' and seeks 'knowledge' of the world, nor are these exactly a sure bulwark against misconceptions and racism of all sorts. But I am concerned here not so much to denounce the essentially pernicious nature of any reduction of another culture to the status of object for one's curiosity or consumption, as to stress how ready the public is to attend to any discourse concerning 'the others', a readiness which is assuredly very ambiguous but which, for this same reason, grows and thus makes more complex the task of those who, professionally, claim to know something about them.

There is in fact, a comparable ambiguity affecting anthropological debate. Some of the above reasons may be held to account for it, but there are others too, which are more closely linked to the history of research and to history itself. This debate turns basically on three points, points that can easily be shown to be closely related if not inextricably confused. It concerns the researchers themselves, the meaning of their presence outside their own countries, and the use that can be made of their work. It concerns the populations that are the object both of an anthropological 'gaze' and of colonial or neo-colonial politics whose consequences run from acculturation through deculturation to ethnocide, even to genocide. Finally, it bears on the general validity of the intellectual schemata that western observers use when investigating different societies. There is no great distance separating actual presence from 'gaze', or 'gaze' from model, and political, deontological and intellectual preoccupations thus find themselves naturally bound together.

Such a confusion of different perspectives would be thoroughly healthy and justifiable if it did not entail risks of which even the best-intentioned observers have no conception. For it can lead to a mystification of the societies in which they are supposedly taking an interest, even if it does not also entail reducing these same societies, either through paying exaggerated tribute to their virtues or through paying insufficient attention to their diversity, to being nothing more than pawns in a debate that primarily concerns western intellectuals.

In France at any rate the anthropological debate turns on an opposition between those who, in one sense or another, are avowed Marxists, and those who repudiate this line of descent. This distinction has nothing to do with functionalist, culturalist or structuralist options, which are not superseded as such, but which no longer dominate the factional disputes between schools and researchers. Given all the appropriate reservations, one could advance the argument that, of those who repudiate Marxism, there must be many who have been intellectually discomforted by the wrongdoings of the Stalinist epoch; they have therefore tended to place in question the very spirit of western logic, as if it were essentially reductive and imperialist, and have valorised the social and intellectual models encountered in different societies, particularly Stateless ones. It has therefore happened, paradoxically enough, that those same people who used to denounce the positioning of a disjuncture between societies with and without a State or with and without writing, a disjuncture that involved defining one group of human societies in terms of the absence of characteristics peculiar to the other group, have come to reinstate this disjuncture. They have not merely reinstated it, however, but have taken it further, and have stressed instead the deficiencies that the key features of western societies with States imply. Put crudely, our societies are thought to have lost the thing that validates the others, namely, authenticity, a word first employed in anthropology by Claude Lévi-Strauss,[2] and regrettably no longer used by him alone.

There have been anthropologists (French for the most part) who, faced

3

with the century's political disillusionments and with the dubious nature of recent theoretical developments, have yielded all too easily to intellectual constructions that have no genuine anchorage in reality. They have thus given laymen the impression that what they are expounding derives from a particular experience and mode of enquiry, when in actual fact they are imposing, in the course of *illustrating* certain exotic facts, a schema, a 'theory' and perhaps a phantasy. One can thus descry in anthropological texts the noble but blurred outline of a savage who, being nearer to nature than we are, must have refused in advance all that oppresses us (the Oedipal triangle, the State, abstraction), and whose trace, memory or testimony one may still find in the Amazonian forests or in the Australian deserts. With the help of fashion (and under pressure from a demand that actually epitomises the unease of an epoch or a society) a greater and greater number of increasingly picturesque savages are paraded before us. These savages die better than we, live better than we; they know better than we do the secrets of both life and death and the mysterious texture of the real, and how to *see* and turn away from the sterile schemata of analytic thought. There is therefore a risk that intellectuals will, in their disillusionment, amplify the current mood of nostalgia and thus reinforce the mystificators' lies. This will lead only to obscurantism.

Can we, then, not hope to hear the genuine voice of others? Born of culture shock and of the clash of unequal forces, syncretic movements and messianic cults proclaim the meaning of a defeat that they can only cancel by superseding: the real object for which the defeated of yesterday quite legitimately search is the secret of the whites' strength and the reasons for the defeat they have suffered. Can the newspapers have captured the full irony or drama of the followers of Lumumba or Mulele believing themselves to be bulletproof if, now that they are dead, we allow ourselves the luxury of believing in the efficacy of their magic? The West knows when and how to exploit doubt or faith for its own purposes. Yet the vision and researches of the defeated[3] were based on reality, and when, in the perhaps still-distant future, their attempts at reconquest have ended, they will grasp from the others (from us) a part of the most critical reason for their defeat. People in black Africa do in fact talk of the lost strength that people of bygone times possessed and that they did not hand on, but they also know that it is gone just like everything else. The more clear-sighted African intellectuals, like Paulin Hountondji, object to every attempt, however generous it might seem, to mark out a separate destiny for their world, as if it has ever been more unanimous, less hierarchised and more 'philosophical' than our own. This, then, is the temptation and the vertigo from which a certain form of anthropology suffers, and in constructing a discipline apart for societies apart, it selects only their past (their 'tradition', their state prior to western aggression) and idealises it.

Anthropology and history

What of the Marxist contribution? Whilst there have been numerous attempts at applying categories like 'mode of production' and 'social formation' to the analysis of societies traditionally studied by ethnographers, there has never been, with one or two exceptions, any systematic endeavour to break with this tradition. Debates internal to Marxism have turned around the question of classes. Marxist anthropologists have asked whether for instance, it was legitimate to talk of the oppositions between elders and juniors in lineage societies in terms of class? Non-Marxists have had a fine time denouncing this problem as typically Europocentrist, and some Marxists have expressed the fear that, in using the term 'class' in too wide a sense (as when one applies it to the different positions occupied in processes of circulation and distribution, for instance, or to reproduction and not to production), one strips it of all operational value. It is common knowledge that, for Marx, class oppositions concern the basic opposition labour/non-labour, some profiting from (exploiting) the surplus labour of others. It is hard to apply a definition of this sort to the reality of African lineage societies, even though they are hierarchised. But is this the most pertinent question? Should we not ask instead if it is possible, from the same anthropological perspective, to undertake the study of a whole range of societal forms, starting not with empirical categories that are always admitted *a priori* (and which the opposition between the disciplines that are supposed to study them, i.e., ethnology and sociology, masks) but with intellectual objects that may be apprehended and constituted through the concrete diversity of societies? The aim here would not be to fix in an artificial synchrony the study of diverse institutional or symbolic forms, but to delineate the real parameters of history. If class relations represent only one of a whole range of power relations, history cannot be identified with the history of class struggle; which is also to say that it does not begin, or end, with the hypothetical establishment of 'classless' societies. In this respect, it is curious to note the emergence of a debate on the existence or otherwise of classes in the present-day socialist societies, a debate not dissimilar to the one whose pertinence some anthropologists have contested when it was applied to lineage societies. In the former situation too, the concept will perhaps have to be over-extended or else renounced.

But non-Marxists (or anti-Marxists), far from mocking or vilifying the Marxists, ought to be grateful to them for maintaining the same categories and for asserting, as they do, the radical difference of pre-industrial societies. It should be said that there is a lofty precedent for all this. Marxist philosophers, even when they are at odds over the meaning or extension of the concept of ideology, are in (implicit) agreement that it should not be applied, or at least not *in toto*, to 'classless' societies. Thus Jacques Rancière[4] reproaches Althusser for his definition of ideology 'in general', as that system of representations which in every society would assure social cohesion at the price of an effect of opacity; but for Althusser himself division into classes

5

adds to the deformation produced by ideology 'in general', the dominating class complicating (over-determining) the general effect of opacity through a mystifying representation of the social system which functions to its profit. In other words, for Althusser (whose definition of class remains traditionally Marxist), classless societies are also without mystification and lie at the innocent end of the ideological spectrum. Rancière goes further, maintaining all ideology is class ideology, and yet he does not deny the existence of classless societies. It is worth pondering the possibility that Marxist philosophers, following in this respect an anthropological tradition that has always paid attention to the integrative functions of the societies it has studied, are effectively assigning one part of humanity to symbolic existence (to representations and to relative harmony) and the other to ideological existence (to manipulations and to struggle). The passage from symbolic to ideological would then be equivalent, on a temporal axis, to the emergence of classes.

One can thus find the same intellectual blank, the same blurred gaze and the same misconceptions in the background of scholarly discourses as characterises popular ethnographic literature. Or, in noble but deceptive terms, there is this same unknowable and unknown quality, one that arouses in many people, along with uncertainty, desire. Anthropological discourse is the less innocent for being part of history; that of others, certainly, since the anthropologist intervened alongside the officer, the administrator and the missionary, but also part of its own history, produced and received by men of a particular epoch and society, in a determinate intellectual and political conjuncture.

One can thus account in part for its difficulties, its regrets, its ambiguities and its predilections. Yet anthropological discourse is also without history or, if you like, outside history. The difficulties it encounters are also strictly intellectual ones, which the diversity neither of cultures in which field-work is done, nor of epochs, nor of theories, will fully explain.

Anthropologists have always had to face two questions bearing on meaning and on function, but have not succeeded in providing any consistent answer to them. The first is, what do the institutions encountered in a society *mean*, given the fact that they are amenable to comparison all over the world; and the second, what use are they? The first question is usually tackled in those anthropological studies which are devoted to the study of symbolic systems, institutions, and beliefs treated as representations. Whether these studies are culturalist, psychoanalytic or structuralist in inspiration, and whether they refer to a culture in its specificity, to drives or to general configurations that occur in the human mind, they are in every case concerned with the expressive value of systems. An entire French tradition undertakes enquiries of this sort. Thus, through works by Marcel Griaule and Germaine Dieterlen, which have unveiled more and more of the intricate and impressive architecture of a system of thought, a cosmogony and a cosmology, the Dogon have acquired a fame that extends far beyond the context of academic anthropology. Lévi-Strauss's works have lent substance to the idea of human nature, by identifying universal unconscious structures beneath the various cultural manifestations of the human mind. Whilst they differ in many respects, these enquiries have in common the fact of being, literally, more anthropological than sociological, more concerned to reveal intellectual mechanisms than to analyse power relations or the functioning of institutions; they favour the study of symbolic production, of symbolic systems such as language, marriage rules, economic relations, science, art and religion, which taken together, for Lévi-Strauss, define a culture.

English-speaking anthropologists have tended to favour the second question, and, more particularly, have concerned themselves with systems of representations only in as much as they serve explicitly, implicitly or unconsciously to further the functioning of a social system. Through a kind of paradox peculiar to the history of anthropology, Durkheim has won more of an audience with the Anglo-Saxons than with the French. If Durkheim was concerned with religion, it was not so much in order to decipher the mark of the human mind at work in the constitution of symbols, as to analyse the efficacy of representation: it is because religion *represents* the social, by means of large gatherings and collective effervescence, that it renders it desirable, or in any case, acceptable. There are two main aspects of the Durkheimian approach. First of all, it treats the 'expressive' value of religion as more important than anything else, in that it represents something other than itself. Secondly, it is concerned with elucidating the secret of symbolic efficacy, with understanding the passage from representation to action. The second aspect is at once the most difficult, the most fragile and the most interesting. This doubtless explains why it is that the first should dominate those anthropological monographs that are more or less Durkheimian in inspiration: the idea that one 'level' of reality represents another (and that one can, for instance, undertake a 'reading' of the 'social level' by means of the 'religious level') is the principle that implicitly informs many such accounts. This idea is not, moreover, peculiar to any one theory, and there are assuredly structuralist, functionalist or Marxist modes of yielding to the temptation of specularity.

The subtler analyses in this area strive to disrupt the circular logic of mirror effects and to give some account of the problems of efficacy. Max Gluckman, for example, strives to show that the tensions that are expressed ritually in 'rituals of rebellion' are real, even if their institutionalised expression is a means of reducing them, and Victor Turner insists on the sensory, biological and organic dimensions of symbolic or ritual activity. In Turner's opinion, these dimensions serve to guarantee the passage from the obligatory to the desirable, whereas Durkheim had seen this same passage as depending on the collective nature of that activity.

7

But because there is no one answer to these two questions the authors who try to answer them are forced (as are those cited above) to diversify their perspectives, to change, more or less consciously, their objectives, or to allow difficulties that stem from the complexity of the real to harden into doctrinal or disciplinary oppositions. For, if it is true that institutions serve a purpose *and* signify, it is also true that the secret of function does not lie in signification, nor vice versa. It is thus not hard for us to distinguish two major orientations in the history of anthropology (and to locate them in accounts of it), one favouring analyses in terms of meaning, symbol, evolution and the human mind, the other favouring analyses in terms of function, ideology, culture and social organisation. One might think that the former would make it easier to elicit relations between individual psyche and social symbolism, and that it would clear a space for psychoanalysis and ethnopsychiatry, whereas the second, despite appearances (and, for instance, Malinowski's disclaimers), would be closer to history. But I would yet again emphasise that these two approaches, each equally interesting and equally necessary, cannot in themselves, whether considered separately or in juxtaposition, be held to give an exhaustive account of the whole of reality. They express a complexity, and also a helplessness, that the best anthropologists, because they are the best, cannot help but recognise, and to which, beyond the avatars of theory, recurrent oscillations in the history of anthropology bear witness.

In one sense there is no history of anthropology, and current debates, even Parisian ones, do nothing more than revive the old, indissociable, irreconcilable and complementary oppositions between the demand on the one hand, that anthropological signification, individuality and human identity be taken into account and, on the other, that sociological meaning, social relations and cultural specificity also be considered. Whilst there is no identity or human individuality that can be apprehended separately from its social determination, neither is there any institution or specific social organisation that does not set in motion a more general symbolism. Particularly revealing, from this point of view, are all those institutions and ceremonies in which, in a language that is always historically and culturally marked, individual destinies and social organisations are decided. The passage from birth to death is thus marked by puberty rites, graduation rites and marriage rites. Or, in a more political and more restricted register, initiation or coronation rites assume, in massively different contexts, irreducibly diverse but nonetheless comparable forms, that both yield meaning sociologically and, anthropologically, work as signs.

This duality lies as much in observed reality as in the mind that does the observing, and this latter is forever condemned to choose between its quarry and the shadow that the quarry casts. On the one hand it treats what is absolutely individual as an abstraction, and social reality as the sole observable reality (Gurvitch's sociology, in this respect, takes this to its logical conclusion, in that the terms 'individual' and 'concrete' are defined as strictly antithetical), while on the other it leaves out economic and social context, and the historical conjuncture, the sole thing to give meaning to the existence of concrete individuals. It permeates or overlaps with all those debates in which, sometimes within the same work, evolutionism and culturalism, functionalism and structuralism, structuralism and Marxism, or even the most recent amalgams of these theoretical options, are opposed.

In another sense anthropology *is* part of history. This is not simply because, as I have already indicated, its problems, concerns and temptations are part of a common heritage. Nor is it just because one would have to be astonishingly blind, when faced with the reality of others, to ignore the relations between force and meaning through which force is opposed to and imposed upon meaning, and each day increasingly so. It is rather because it participates, even if those who practise it are unaware of this, and even if its specificity as a discipline is thus sacrificed, in the advance of forms of knowledge which, in all areas, are identified with the march of history. One can doubtless assert, without therefore being naive or lapsing into paradox, that the more aware anthropology becomes of its involvement in history the more chance it has of eluding its own historical determinations and, if I may put it like this, of not alienating itself from itself. This is both because its existence as a discipline, and the places that feature as objects of ethnographic observation, are products of history, and because as a scientific practice it is also a historical practice, and one that is rarely more and sometimes less innocent than any other.

If one considers the intelligence and wealth of ancient philosophies, or the remarkable intricacy of 'exotic' social systems which, from the Inca empire to Australian nomadic culture, from African chiefdoms to Indian kingdoms, bear witness to the ingenuity and diversity of human genius, to its admirable capacity for combining the sacred, the political and the social, one is sometimes tempted to think that the notion of progress has no more meaning in the human sciences than in poetry. If one reads those contemporary authors who are forever rediscovering America one is all the more likely to be tempted in this way. But one should sometimes be on one's guard against both the *a priori* from which such temptations stem, and the confusions to which they testify. The *a priori* here is that of absolute relativism and complete scepticism. It implies that one system is as good as another, provided it has its proper coherence, and it may well constitute the first stage of a reactionary programme whose equivalent is to be found in the sort of political discourse that follows on from or amplifies the assertion that previous systems had, when all is said and done, more coherence and more meaning. The virtues of the race, the riches of the soil, and the meaning of the compact between man and man are always placed in the past, and whilst these themes may

9

constitute the bare bones of reactionary argument, they are always introduced, set in place and articulated through a sceptical discourse that, under cover of a general denunciation, strives above all to devalue the meaning of the present. As the dark side of the idea of progress, 'sceptical' discourse lies (both with respect to its object and with respect to its scope) when it presents itself as the sad truth of a world without history.

This discourse appeals very directly to anthropologists, and in this respect it is clear that its intellectual problems (evolution/diffusion, meaning/function, function/history) overlap with political ones. And if one takes it for granted that anthropologists should not, for all that, seek to be optimists or pessimists, believers or unbelievers, one would also do well to remember that they ought not to smuggle in, for the purpose of analysing some societies, criteria that they had ruled out when judging others. The example that I will now cite illustrates very clearly what risks the anthropologist may be induced to run, when he deems that he is simply applying himself to specific analyses.

In Amerindian society torture has been practised in a manner that is at once subtle and extremely codified; we have, for instance, accurate accounts of the ritual in which the Tupinamba put their prisoners of war to death.[5] These prisoners might well have spent several years with their enemies, having settled down and intermarried with them, before being executed and then eaten, all according to a ceremonial procedure that was meticulously organised. They knew when this event was to take place, accepted it, and shared their conquerors' and executioners' value system and sense of honour to such an extent that, if the chroniclers are to be believed, they never sought to run away. Claude Lévi-Strauss, in one of his lectures at the Collège de France, observed in passing that practices of this kind are radically different from those in which torture is used in modern western societies to extort confessions. It is always pertinent, in this respect, to recall that no society is more 'savage' than any other, but that it is not therefore necessary to compare the incomparable. One can in fact find an equivalent, in the western tradition, for the system of shared values that the Tupinamba example illustrates; as, for instance, in the 'rules of war', in the implicit code of mutual respect ordering relations between a prisoner and the person responsible for him, and in the saluting of the courageous adversary that comprises the background of Renoir's film, *La Grande Illusion*. Neither a spy nor a deserter is shot without decorum and observation of the rules. From another angle we find in non-western societies cases of violent practices that are explicitly meant to extort a confession. The various forms of ordeal work quite ingloriously on the body of the accused, and it is clearly with these and with other related practices that it is appropriate to compare the punishments and tortures of the dark history of the West.

Each 'rehabilitation', however useful, is nevertheless liable to result in an idealisation of its object and, what is more, in a surreptitious change of object. The observer who disregards his lack of knowledge about other societies and uses their rediscovered values as a yardstick against which to measure his own society's shortcomings is therefore walking into a trap. For what appears to be an anti-ethnocentrism is in fact a constant of our literary and philosophical tradition, and turns out to be, in the last analysis, one of the most imperialist of ethnocentrisms. Thus today we find the *Anti-Oedipus* philosophers joining forces with Bataille, and, beyond him, with Nietzsche, in order to contrast our societies, in which abstraction, arbitrariness and axiomatic notions dominate, with societies featuring notions of the concrete, of meaning, and of code. Although they were not the first to make this convenient and somewhat startling detour, some ethnographers have followed it and, like the philosophers, proceed by way of Amazonia in order to speak of Stalinism, thus projecting the shadow of our own terrors and phantasies on to a magnified image of others, and placing anthropology inside our own history.

I want now to revert to the question of progress in the human sciences, and to the areas in which this notion is applicable: that of the societies studied and that of the discipline by means of which they are studied. It is certainly true that, for an anthropologist, one social system is worth as much as another, and has, in a sense, the same degree of dignity as all the others, and that what the observer sees as potential aberrations are only the manifestations of a more complex rationality. Whatever progress ethnography has enjoyed this century is attributable to just such attempts at eliminating categories like 'pre-logical' and 'irrational', as well as simplistic evolutionism and naive ethnocentrism. But it is also clear that absolute relativism, or the culturalism that has it that each type of society should be evaluated in terms of its 'style', are not tenable positions. There are two reasons for this; first, because societies change, and because the reasons for (and manifestations of) this change are themselves problematic (in this sense history is part of anthropology); and second, because the observer, however objective he seeks to be, does not consider himself to be apolitical, or at least not where his own society is concerned. How, in laying claim to absolute relativism, would he be able to judge his own society? And if he were to draw the line at analysing his own society, how would he avoid constituting the others as a kind of natural-history gallery, outside of social history and politics? All societies codify men's relations with each other, their relation to the earth and to production, the relations between the sexes and the generations, and these different codes do in themselves encourage, in the observers' eyes, the making of comparisons (in this sense anthropology is part of history).

It is not clear why a certain geographical, sociological or historical distance should make it impossible for us to pass judgement on a society, since we make value judgements about the societies and political regimes that

11

surround us. Nor is it clear why the 'field' (in the anthropological sense) should become restricted to debates in which the intellectual categories of the 'observers' are projected ineluctably and in the most aggressively ethnocentric manner conceivable. There are all too many instances of this sort of abuse, as much in the economic literature (where formalists seek to rediscover in 'primitive' economies the defining features of a liberal economy) as in mission ethnographies (where missionaries seek to discover in local systems of representations the idea of a single God and the blurred outline of a potential Christianity). If, through the use of precise criteria, societies can still be differentiated, this differentiation is not made in order to set up an intolerably hypocritical prize list referring to those forms that have occurred historically, but in order to eliminate the supposedly antagonistic terms of that alternative in which the demands for objectivity and for meaning are pitted against each other, as are, in a certain manner, ethnographic impartiality and the meaning of history.

Some feminists, particularly in America,[6] are clearly aiming at this and, in denouncing the masculine bias of the existing ethnographic literature, seek to reassess the man/woman relation in certain societies. But one would have cause to be wary of the teleology of this endeavour if it tended to follow primarily the warped logic of an apparent anti-ethnocentrism and, in order to denounce the man/woman relation in our society, idealised it in those societies that are different from ours. We should be as much on our guard against blindly endorsing the idea of the objective progress of societies, held by the optimistic and ethnocentric evolutionist thinkers of the nineteenth century, for this would be to scorn what a century of anthropology has taught us, as we should be against caricaturing it and thus giving no answer to the question that it continues to raise. We will, more precisely, be eager to know if anthropology and history might now enable us to discern more clearly the status of the individual (or more exactly, the individual statuses) in different types of societies, where the notion of individual status implies a set of relations with the immediate social, natural and supernatural surroundings. Whilst acknowledging the contradictions of history or the monstrous nature of modern totalitarianisms, it is neither excusable to disregard the extent and purchase of power constraints in Stateless societies, nor inconceivable to emphasise the positive elements in what we, whilst denouncing its imperialist and capitalist foundation, term the globalisation of 'culture'. An assertion of this sort is bound to shock, especially coming from an anthropologist, at a time when the urgency of protecting the different cultural inheritances against the blind standardisation of the modern imperialisms has been particularly clearly asserted. But I am not questioning that such things are happening, nor the urgency of investigating them; rather that their occurrence is something that has to be taken into account, along with the rest, as one of the features and doubtless one of the dialectical mainsprings of modern State societies.

Many, refusing the meaning of history, are nevertheless tempted to see in the modern State's forms the end of history and of the world, forms that haunted and obsessed our now lost liberties and were never sufficiently contested. We must refuse this temptation, for history does not end with us.

If it is true that the history of mankind, which has not been without its shocks (precisely because it is the history of their struggles), is essentially the history of a gradual disalienation and of a relative liberation from the fetishism of institutions, of power and of the economy (a disalienation and liberation whose progress is always threatened and that is limited in extent, for the idea of a society that would be identified simply as a collection of individuals remains unthinkable and unworkable), anthropology must still have a critical meaning and function. This is so even when it must in the end (which is still a long way off) record the respective weight of the different determinations that condition social life; and, having admitted as a requirement, as obvious as it is inconvenient to put into practice and difficult to formulate, the theoretical necessity of interdisciplinarity, it must be dissolved into a social science that is at the last reconciled with itself, and in which meaning and function, symbol and history are no longer opposed.

1

The anthropological circle

Two axes and four poles

The history of anthropology, such as we learn it in manuals or in theoretical argument in monographs and essays, is always presented in the form of alternatives or of confrontations. Since its basic problem is always that of combining the same and the other in their most varied aspects (human identity and cultural specificity, culture and cultures, the unconscious and practices, the individual and society), one can see that behind these debates, however technical they may seem, philosophical options are invariably, in however approximate or parodic a form, being delineated.

Anthropology has neither resolved nor excluded the problem of the status of the other, for it is both its torment and its justification. Where societies are concerned, there is not an unlimited number of possible theoretical positions. Either one considers the other as the same, but deferred or delayed (this is evolutionism), or one considers the various others as so many irreducibly different entities (this is culturalism, a doctrine that fits very well with a functionalist analysis of the different components of each society), or again one considers this otherness as relative (and this relativity no longer has to be referred to a chronological dimension, on to which the evolutionary development of societies is mapped) and situates identity on the side of the unconscious (this is the structuralist procedure). I have, of course, given a particularly rigid formulation of these possibilities here, and actual anthropological procedures do in fact attempt, in varying degrees, to reconcile or combine them. It is just at this point, moreover, that the difficulties begin. In as much as they no longer appear to be mutually exclusive options, they become obvious and, in as much as they become obvious, it is difficult to place them in relation to each other.

I would note, first of all, that, however crude these formulations regarding the status of the other are, they are still quite current and figure, for instance, in certain authors' phrasing of the problem of the State and of capitalism. One is quite within one's rights in qualifying the anthropology of difference, as illustrated by writers like Jaulin, as neo-culturalist, to the extent that such

14

authors make it a priority to try and mark those thresholds that define one culture as irreducibly different from another. Similarly, those who, inspired by Deleuze, respect the divisions established by Morgan (savagery, barbarism, civilisation) can be described as neo-evolutionist, even if they reverse the value judgement as to the degree of 'civilisation' of each of these stages. One can also identify an implicit problem of difference in the analyses, touched upon in the introduction, that Marxist philosophers like Althusser and Rancière make of the notion of ideology. While Althusser distinguishes between ideology in general, which is necessary for the functioning of society as a whole, and ideology in class society, which is manipulated by the dominant class and is explicitly mystifying, Rancière[1] objects that the concept of ideology only has meaning in relation to the class struggle, that all ideology is class ideology, and that the ideological domain, far from constituting a necessary and in some respects 'neutral' aspect of social functioning in general, is part and parcel of the historical domain of the class struggle. But both of them admit, without turning a hair, that there is no problem of ideology in classless societies, either because, to be more specific, it is not posed in the same terms (Althusser would see religion as being the pure and primitive form of ideology in general), or because it is not posed at all (Rancière does not breathe a word about it, even though he does not deny the existence of classless societies). This handling of the question contrasts oddly with the attempts of Marxist anthropologists to apply categories like 'mode of production' to the analysis of pre-capitalist societies, and thereby to qualify the difference between types of social formation, in order the better to understand it.

The intellectual necessity to think of the other as both different and identical accounts for some difficulties, but a number of additional considerations aggravate these even further. First, the category of 'the other' is applicable not only to distinctions between different societies but also to distinctions internal to each of them. If one thinks of societies in culturalist terms one does, in the last analysis, eliminate the problem of a society's internal differences, and this serves to justify all those idealisations of primitive society that mark our philosophical history and characterise, in particular, certain aspects of current thought. On the other hand, if one pays exclusive attention to the manner in which differences internal to a society operate, useful and valuable though this may be, it can cause one to eliminate, at a certain level of analysis, a mode of reflection which is nonetheless necessary for a comparison between different societies and for a consideration of the development of each society. One would thus, in both respects, be eliminating history. It is therefore fairly remarkable that Malinowski, whose investigation of the Trobriand islanders can properly be said to be the earliest and best example of the anthropological monograph, and of the functionalist theory that informs it, should have been led to consider all approaches involving history as pointless and, so to speak, trivial, in the light of a sociology whose main task was always seen to be the explanation of integrative mechanisms. But it is even more remarkable that he should have been joined in this by Lévi-Strauss, whose structuralism requires a plurality of sociological cases in order to highlight the unconscious structures of the human mind at work in social life, and who describes as a 'truism' the assertion that every society functions but who, for all that, accords no scientific privilege to the study of change.

Bearing these difficulties in mind, I will now try to see exactly what form they assume in the anthropological tradition. Not, I repeat, because I am trying to write yet another history of anthropology, but rather because it is a question of describing in broad strokes the intellectual tools that anthropologists today have at their disposal, which must clearly affect the manner in which they approach and carry out their work. If anthropology is, to some degree, without a history, it is because anthropological modes of thought have always tended to be articulated and constructed in relation to two intellectual axes, axes which in fact served to orient the actual founders of the discipline. By the actual founders I mean those authors whose thought still serves as a support for the most recent theoretical positions or hypotheses (Morgan, Durkheim, Malinowski), and those who would seem to have advanced their work or provided illustrative examples for it (Tylor, Boas, Lévy-Bruhl, Radcliffe-Brown).

In making this distinction I do not mean to slight the work of the second category of authors, but to stress the still vital and controversial nature of the first. Thus, in an essay written in 1970,[2] Emmanuel Terray recalls the influence of Morgan on certain aspects of Marxist thought and reassesses the relevance of his formulations for the areas that preoccupy economic anthropologists. Durkheim is the semi-official inspiration for the studies English anthropologists have made of questions of representation and religion: I have in mind here the most astute ones (by Victor Turner and Mary Douglas). The fact, moreover, that he still figures in certain Marxist polemics demonstrates that his work is still current. Thus when Rancière, in a work cited above, rebukes Althusser for his concept of ideology in general, he gives a name and ascribes an origin to this supposed sin of bourgeois idealism, that is, Durkheim. It remains to be seen whether employment of the language of class struggle (one ideology per class) does not end up restoring a problematic of difference that is incapable of accounting for the social fact and, beyond that, for the why and wherefore of class struggle.

Durkheim is also still relevant, though less directly so, to certain authors within the French intellectual and university tradition who refuse to make a distinction between anthropology and sociology and therefore between one part of humanity, to be studied qualitatively, and another, to be studied quantitatively. It is significant that one can ascribe a Durkheimian origin to the work of both Balandier and Lévi-Strauss, for whilst the former opts for a sociology in which no restriction is placed either on its empirical object (the more or less primitive nature of the societies studied), or on the number of 'levels' of reality to be considered (holding, rather, that the sacred may well be the 'language' of the political), Lévi-Strauss's work is, as Bourdieu has complained, Durkheimian to the degree that it attends more to 'structured' than to 'structuring' structure, to the sociology of knowledge than to the sociology of action, to symbol than to function.

As for Malinowski, whose personality seems to have provoked an irritation of which one can still, curiously enough, find traces in the history of anthropology,[3] he has had the curious privilege of being the object of lively criticism by his colleagues and successors for many years. It is doubtless because the positions that he took up were always extreme ones, and because he advocated analysis of the factors that work to bring about a society's integration as cultural totality, that he is situated by preference on the side of culturalism and difference. It is for these reasons also that he has been the object of sometimes divergent, sometimes combined, criticism, from the partisans of history and from the partisans of structure, from Lowie, Gluckman, Lévi-Strauss and Leach, and, of course, from the psychoanalysts, who have never been convinced by his assertion that the Oedipus complex is absent in Trobriand society. But the functionalist analysis of society has other virtues, and Paul Mercier, in his *Histoire de l'anthropologie*, is quite right to point out that the analysis of *kula*-type commerce in the islands on the eastern coast of New Guinea, in that it demonstrates the close interlocking of the various aspects of social and cultural life, represents a reformulation of Marcel Mauss's 'total social fact'. I would simply observe that, in addition to this, it provides a very suggestive outline of certain aspects of substantivist economic analysis. Malinowski's theoretical ambition thus explains and justifies the place of his work, however polemical it is and however much it has been contested, at the cross-roads of all the original attempts in anthropological analysis that have marked the last few decades of research.

These authors may still, however, in spite of their diversity, be ordered in terms of the two axes mentioned. The first axis features the notions of symbol and function, considered as two opposed and contradictory poles. One can seek out a society's statements on humanity or on society in general, and one can choose to study the logic of its language or the unconscious of its practices, and thus always treat meaning as an extension of symbols. Or else one can study a given society as being, in the last analysis, an organic totality. One will then examine the logic of processes of integration and the internal links between different modes of organisation or expression, and one will look for meaning in terms of one's understanding of function.

A second axis features the notions of evolution and culture, also considered as two opposed and mutually contradictory poles. If one concentrates on the features that define a culture as specific, one by and large rules out the transformational possibilities that it enjoys. Anthropology's task is therefore seen as being that of understanding the irreducible character of a given culture, or of its 'dominant tendencies', to revive a term from Ruth Benedict's writing, rather than that of discerning the manner in which it undergoes transformation. In the last analysis it involves reducing culture to integration and to 'style' (the combination of 'features'), and history to the chance diffusion of cultural 'features', this notion applying as much to a technical invention (like the bow and arrow or pottery) as to social customs like a rule of patrilocal residence or of mother-in-law avoidance. Here too it is hard to imagine any convergence between an approach in which practitioners seek to delimit particular configurations and an approach in which they seek to identify the elementary principles of 'the psychic unity of mankind' in each and every cultural fact. The latter expression derives from Bastian, a German scholar (1826–1903) who boldly anticipated subsequent advances in pre-structuralism, applied anthropology and psychology and thus earned, along with Tylor's esteem, the forgetfulness of history.

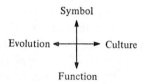

If one considers the symbol–function and evolution–culture axes one will discern fairly obvious convergences and also other, more obscure, configurations. Culture and function would seem to combine more easily than function and evolution. Likewise, symbol and evolution, in that they both appeal to the same category of universality, may be more easily combined than culture and symbol. The employment of the category 'symbol' tends, by definition, to imply that the culture using it may be compared with others, and this allows one to qualify that irreducible and finally ineffable character in terms of which, for want of the capacity to define itself, a society's spirit, style or soul is expressed.

Evolution, culture, symbol

It is nevertheless quite possible to conceive of all the different combinations' being attempted, and we do find them in operation, in one form or another, in the writings of the founders of anthropology, who are, by the same token, still relevant to us. The tensions that necessarily result from trying to refer at once to the poles of the two axes and to the two axes themselves, and which may even give rise to contradictions, can perhaps be most clearly discerned in Morgan's work. Let me define these tensions more closely. We know that in *Ancient Society* (1877), a work which had a strong influence on Marx and Engels, Morgan distinguished three different states (savagery, barbarism, civilisation) that were defined in terms of the presence or absence of a certain number of features (the state of savagery precedes pottery, the state of barbarism is also the age of ceramics, writing epitomises the state of civilisation), each being subdivided into three levels (lower, middle, higher), and each level being defined in terms of a specific combination of features.

In *The History of Ethnological Theory*,[4] some of whose analyses I will follow here, Robert Lowie stresses the areas in which Morgan is ignorant and protests against some of the *a priori* assumptions of his theoretical framework. Thus we are told that Morgan, because he holds that the bow and arrow correspond with the upper level of the state of savagery, classes the Polynesians, who have neither bow nor arrow, as being of the same level (middle) as Australian hunters and gatherers (lower than the 'rudest' North American Indians), even though they are extremely advanced in horti-cultural terms. The very idea of a prize list of this sort is bound to surprise us nowadays, though not merely because of Lowie's factual criticisms, which bear essentially on the excessive prominence accorded to certain classifica-tory criteria. These criticisms are, nevertheless, extremely important, for three reasons: they are pertinent, they could well be applied to some of the more fashionable meta-anthropological outpourings, and they indicate difficulties integral to the intellectual schema of the two axes. Thus, when Morgan tells us that there can be no monarchy prior to the state of civilisa-tion, as characterised by the emergence of writing, and that monarchy is incompatible with a clan system, his analysis is contradicted by numerous examples of African kingdoms in which writing is not employed and in which the clan system has not disappeared.

But even today one can still find assertions inspired and informed by an attitude of intellectual retreat, which, though aspiring to be the inverse of the smug evolutionism of the nineteenth century, represents both its exact replica and its darker side. The authors posit almost unmediated modes of communication that would correspond with the first forms of intersubjec-tivity and sociability, while more abstract modes of communication, writing first of all, would accompany the increasing autonomy of political institu-tions. This evolutionist pessimism may, moreover, be coupled with a Mani-chaean diffusionism, in which the sins of abstraction and writing, like the as-sociated ones of universalism and imperialism, are considered as being first and foremost the sins of western, Judaeo-Christian civilisation. This denun-ciation stems as much from neo-evolutionists like Pierre Clastres as from neo-culturalists like Robert Jaulin. Like their ancestors, they want to have their cake and eat it, and the authors of *Anti-Oedipus*, fully aware of the possibility of a contradiction at this point, have given it, along with their

19

philosophical guarantee, the appearance of reason, by lightheartedly combining chance and necessity, or, in the old language, diffusion and evolution. The savages, they tell us, tried to ward off the State's inexorable emergence by combating its rise 'from within', only to find it rearing up all of a sudden from outside, in the form of the blond warriors so dear to Nietzsche. Behind such metaphors there lie contradictions, and behind contradictions the old anthropological alternative (evolution or diffusion), one that the founding ancestors of the subject had confronted, and of which the text-books speak.

When Morgan treats the problem of the State, he is faced, as so often, with the difficulty of preserving the evolutionary sequence whilst, at the same time, respecting the specific combination of features that go to make up a culture. Through the notion of feature, and that of stage, itself qualified, a reconciliation between the need for a functional analysis (only certain combinations of features are possible) and the need for an analysis of the meaning (the direction and significance) of evolution tends to occur. But the sometimes glaring failures of Morgan's method, in contrast to his intuitions and inspired analysis, point very clearly to the dangers and setbacks incurred when navigating just by sculling. We can in fact see that Morgan sometimes resists analyses in terms of functional specificities, and emphasises the logic and evolution of particular symbolic systems such as kinship, and sometimes qualifies the notion of evolution by emphasising the diffusion or transmission of cultural features.

If one were to confine oneself to particular aspects of Morgan's work, one would in fact take the evolutionist emphasis to be the most pronounced element. Given the postulate that 'the experience of humanity has always followed almost identical paths' and the 'universal' law that patrilineal systems derive necessarily from matrilineal ones, Morgan concludes that Greece and Rome must have been matrilineal at some point in their history. An assertion of this sort implies that matrilineality may be thought of on its own, independently of other aspects of social life, and therefore in a resolutely non-functionalist perspective. Here diffusion bails out evolution. The peoples of northern Canada have borrowed the bow and arrow but, in other respects, are 'middle' savages; primitive peoples will often borrow pottery without therefore acceding to barbarism.

But this appeal to diffusion may be more systematic, and may thus limit the scope of Morgan's more important discoveries. Amongst these one should include his account of the principal features of a classificatory kinship system (as represented in *Systems of Consanguinity and Affinity*, 1871), the very idea of a comparative study of systems of terminology, and, in particular, the bringing to light of the Crow and Omaha systems of terminology. In order to make my exposition clearer, and for the benefit of the lay reader, I will recall that a crucial advance was made in anthropology when six (and only six) systems of kinship terminology were brought to light for all

human societies.[5] This demonstration did in itself represent a structuralist
or, if you like, a universalist approach to the analysis of societies, whereas
since then the general drift of anthropological reflection, including the
structuralist kind, has been to deny the existence of any necessary link
between types of terminology, descent and alliance, or, to be more precise,
to admit that it has not succeeded in establishing the nature of this link. This
assertion ought itself, however, to be qualified; it has to be acknowledged
that almost all the known systems of Crow terminology accompany matrilineal descent systems, and almost all the known systems of Omaha terminology accompany patrilineal descent systems, while cognatic kinship
forms tend to be linked to other systems of terminology.

Although Morgan has opened up potentially fruitful avenues of exploration here, his methodological eclecticism lessens their effectiveness. Thus, on
the one hand, his diffusionist interpretation of culture harms the more fruitful
aspects of his evolutionist approach, whilst, on the other hand, he restricts
the potential scope of his discovery of symbolic logics as much through a
narrowly functionalist interpretation of symbolic realities as through a
singularly rigid use of the evolutionist schema. Robert Lowie observes that,
in the treatment of two major problems, Morgan's 'parallelism' (this term
meant in the nineteenth century the theory according to which all societies
would evolve in conformity with the same law and by passing through the
same stage) is replaced by its exact antithesis; these problems are those of
the clan and of kinship terminology. If he in fact considers clan[6] organisation
to be a universal for all societies at a given stage, he nevertheless posits a
unique origin for the complex principle according to which certain blood
relations would be systematically recognised as blood relations to the
exclusion of others. The concept's diffusion would be due to an ever-increas-
ing recognition of the genetic benefits of marriage outside the clan. As for
kinship systems, they are spread by means of migrations, and one therefore
has to attribute an identical origin, because they class certain relatives in
the same way, to Hawaiians and to Zulus, to the Tamils of India and to the
Iroquois of New York State. Theoretical aberrations of this sort were very
quickly denounced as such. Thus Lowie observes that, in this respect, the
Australians class certain kinfolk in the same manner as the Iroquois, that
the Iroquois systems (whose terminologies, it should be remembered, are
very exactly recorded by Morgan, who thus provides the means for criticising his own theory) are not uniform, and that some amongst them re-
semble the Polynesian type. We do not therefore conclude that Australians
and Polynesians belong to the same race or that some Iroquois are Polynesians.

One therefore finds in Morgan's writing a very simple evolutionist schema
(societies evolve from promiscuity to monogamy) which is in contradiction
with a highly systematic usage of diffusionist hypotheses. But this would

21

seem to be the expression of a deeper contradiction or, if one prefers, the displacement on to the evolution–culture axis of a debate which belongs on the function–symbol axis. It is in fact the definition of function which is the problem in Morgan, for, whilst he delineates an apparently very structural conception of kinship, in which there is very little concern to link it to the other institutions or systems in a given society, he ties a very utilitarian conception of the functionality of the real to a very redundant conception of the functionalism of analysis. By 'functionality of the real' I mean that, for Morgan, the reason for the clan's existence and success as an institution lies in the improvement of the race (though he is not concerned to work out how this might be observed or analysed; nor does he trouble to check to see if clans and exogamy always go together – which is in fact far from being the case). By 'functionalism of analysis' I mean that Morgan sees identity of terminology as entailing identity of function. If in Polynesia there is a single term designating both father and mother's brother, that must mean both that the brother can copulate with his sister, and that the system of terminology is simple, and therefore, in evolutionist terms, more ancient.

It should be apparent that the whole of Morgan's theory depends on a very narrowly dichotomised and specular interpretation of the real/language and real/symbol relations, that it makes a radical distinction between the real and what is supposed to express it or represent it, and that it asserts implicitly that there is nothing more in the representative than is in the represented. It is because Morgan separates levels of observation whilst at the same time being incapable of thinking of their relation as anything other than an immediately transparent one, that he does not give any actual heuristic value to the notion of function, and it is because the evidence shows that one cannot locate this transparency in all cultures that he appeals to diffusion. The latter assists evolutionist analysis in its attempts to account for irregularities in the real. In other words, Morgan, failing to account for the real in terms of functions, appeals to diffusionism, which clashes with his evolutionist option. The difficulty which thus appears on the culture–evolution axis actually stems from a reduction of the notion of function to that of symbol, and of that of symbol to that of cultural feature. A culture is composed of 'features' which, except in case of accident, reflect one another. A society's meaning and the significance of its language and symbols can thus refer only to its state and level. Morgan's priority is thus to reconcile and combine symbol and evolution.

Evolution, culture, function

One can make the same sorts of observation about Tylor as about Morgan, in so far as, in *Researches*, he uses, either in turn or simultaneously, two explanatory principles: the historical (diffusionist) relation and the concept of psychic unity. But his originality lies in his attempt to give a meaning to the notion of function by establishing correlations and statistical checks. He is thus able to demonstrate the existence of a link between a number of features, for instance exogamy and Iroquois kinship terminology. Lowie congratulates him in this respect for having brought about the 'substitution of the mathematical concept of function for the metaphysical concept of cause'. However, Tylor comes up against the same difficulty as Morgan: how can one reconcile an analysis in terms of evolution with an analysis in terms of cultural specificity? He tries to achieve this by deducing a temporal sequence from statistical correlations. Lowie presents several of these attempts and gives a very pertinent critique of them. Here I will discuss only his correlation between the *couvade*[7] and types of descent system. Tylor tries both to establish this correlation and to demonstrate that 'matriarchal' societies precede 'patriarchal' societies. He in fact distinguishes between three different types of society. Matriarchal society is a little ambiguously named, since its definition refers to relations between men, even when they pass via women. It is defined by a principle of descent (matrilineal), a principle of authority (avuncular), and a principle of inheritance (nepotic), whereas patriarchal society is defined by a patrilineal, paternal authority, and a filial mode of inheritance. In the intermediate systems these different characteristics are more or less mixed. Tylor wonders what relationship a particular custom like the *couvade* bears to these three types and sets up correlations on the basis of the material available to him. He can find no case in which the *couvade* is associated with a matrilineal society, twenty cases associated with intermediate societies, and eight cases associated with patrilineal societies. From this he deems it fair to conclude that the matriarchal 'level' precedes the others, since, according to the opposite hypotheses, it would be in matrilineal societies that one would find 'survivals' of the *couvade*.

Lowie quite rightly observes that Tylor demonstrates nothing beyond what he had presupposed. What observation actually reveals is not 'levels' or evolutionary stages, but combinations of features and positive or negative correlations between the particularities of different systems; any chronological significance that these correlations may have is asserted rather than demonstrated. The evolutionist hypothesis is necessary if one is to interpret certain correlations as survivals, but the discovery of such correlations does not in itself refer to anything more than configurations that lack a temporal dimension. For Tylor, function (in the sense of a necessary link, statistically registered) has to be reconciled with, and referred to, evolution; here too it is a question of the evolution–culture axis, but the initial difficulty stems from the uncertainty which, in spite of appearances, affects the notion of function.

The difficulties are fundamental ones, and still of relevance to us. Lowie rebukes Tylor for applying the evolutionist framework quite indiscriminately both to elements of material culture and to 'elements of non-material culture associated with values'. But where does the notion of culture begin and where does it end? Establet[8] some years ago criticised the use that American culturalists have made of it, observing that for them everything from material base to superstructure refers to culture, whose domain is therefore not specified; to distinguish 'values' that guide people's actions, as Linton advocates, seemed to him to provide a more workable theory. I will simply point out, for the time being, that the distinctions between institutions and values (a distinction to which Establet's position may, as a first approximation, be assimilated, and which implies, as still more obvious, the distinction between the material and non-material aspects of a culture) is all the more easily maintained in so far as it considers the rigid Marxist schema of infrastructure and the various superstructural levels as self-evident. The difficulties that 'structuralist' Marxists have had in accounting for problems of ideological and symbolic efficacy, or quite simply in giving some status to the notion of ideology (a difficulty to which the already-cited debate between Althusser and Rancière on 'ideology in general' and class ideology testifies), show clearly enough that the notions of culture, ideology and imaginary have not yet been sufficiently analysed and aligned with each other, and we are therefore not yet in a position to condemn culturalism for its totalising ambitions.

One can in fact argue that the conception of a culture as an assemblage of 'features' owes its weakness, from the sociological point of view, to the analytic prejudices it contains. It is therefore perhaps because Morgan and Tylor are so attached to the idea of cultural features that they are incapable of analysing culture either in terms of symbols or in terms of function. Culture as a set of features is understood neither by reference to a logic of the human, which would in the last analysis provide a ground for the logic of symbolic relations, nor by reference to social functions of integration. For Tylor, as for Morgan, contradictions occurring on the evolution–culture axis may only be reconciled to the extent that culture is not defined in terms of an integration model. In the end their analysis rests more on symbol than on function, but symbols are for them nothing more than empty signifiers which only derive their meaning through coming into relation, in a partial and statistical way, with signifiers of the same order. 'Stages' or 'levels' of development thus work as indices, in the context of a development model which has Victorian society as its apogee, but they have no capacity at all to define what is or is not sociologically significant. The *couvade* is only deemed interesting in so far as it has a strong correlation with bilaterality, a lesser correlation with patrilineality and a non-existent correlation with matrilineality. As for these systems themselves, their only interest lies in the possibility of situating them in relation to each other on a chronological axis.

Only the functionalists will end up drawing any positive lessons from the fact that symbolic (or other) relations are also, above all, human and social practices. These conclusions also entail certain intellectual risks, but because we are not ourselves totally immersed in the logic of stages and combinations of features it is hard for us to understand to what degree it might be sane to repudiate history, a refusal which defines the originality of Malinowski's work. Nor can we quite comprehend how it was that Durkheim's claim that sociology should be 'independent' inaugurated a new stage in sociological theory, as did the notion of 'representation', which, however much it is criticised, allows us to define the relationship between the different aspects of social life as being one of meaning.

Symbol, function

Durkheim's work may be said to represent, on two counts, a critical moment in the development of sociological enquiry. It is an attempt to define the appropriate degree of 'independence' that sociology ought to enjoy, thus raising a definitional problem which is not yet resolved, but which is nonetheless an integral part of every anthropological problematic. In addition, it sets up a distinction and a link between the profane and the sacred which raises the problem of *representation* as a sociological concept. In *The Rules of Sociological Method* (1894) Durkheim asserts that psychology is of as little use to the ethnographer as are physics and chemistry in explaining organic facts. Here it is worth noting that he was writing at a period in which there was no biological, animal or vegetable chemistry, no chemotherapy, and it is perhaps just as well for the future of the human sciences that it was so. The idea of a separate development for the various disciplines certainly has a great methodological value at any given moment (and this, let me add, is still the case in the field of the human sciences), but it cannot be considered as anything other than a 'provisional morality'. For one has to be aware that, in the end or indeed in principle, there can be no contradiction between 'natural' and 'cultural' definitions of man (who is always already cultural and social, yet remains natural and psychological also) any more than there can be a contradiction between a society's sociological and historical reality. It seems to me that, in this respect, the 'complementarist' approach, as it has been defined by George Devereux[9] in the field of ethnopsychiatry, provides a very fruitful object of study but an extremely limited project, in so far as the partition separating ethnographic and psychological approaches is supposed to be radically, definitively and essentially watertight. One cannot acknowledge the unity of one's empirical object without postulating an eventual unity of scientific object and approach.

But for Durkheim the independence of sociology has primarily a methodological value: 'The determining causes of a social fact should be sought amongst the preceding social facts and not amongst states of individual consciousness.' The method itself validates the empirical reality of the group and the notions of representation and of relation. Hence everything social is composed of representations and produced by means of representations, and it is the relation between these representations that constitutes the sociologist's object of analysis. Durkheim, like Tylor, is evolutionist, but he is more insistent about the non-lineality of evolution and the possibility of distinct types of development. He sometimes protests against the fact that some argue as if those people known as savages formed an undifferentiated and homogenous whole.

The idea of pluri-evolutionism is certainly stimulating and enables one to avoid being enclosed, from the outset, in an essentially sterile schema, or being trapped in the evolution–culture contradiction; which is doubtless why it has enjoyed an enthusiastic revival over the last few years in the United States. There is always some point, moreover, in criticising the myth of a savage society that is always and everywhere identical to itself, since our phantasies, when they take on a nostalgic form, allow it to spring up again and again. This criticism does help one to avoid denouncing (what is present and what is here) whilst seeming to describe (what existed formerly or elsewhere). It is therefore the attention that Durkheim pays in his analyses to particular, synchronic and social data that prevents them from being too much affected by the *a priori* assumptions of an evolutionist schema – some of whose most contested aspects he does, however, accept (as, for instance, the priority of matrilineality over patrilineality).

It is no coincidence that the most relevant of Durkheim's works is still *The Elementary Forms of the Religious Life* (1912). All the elements necessary for a theory of the social fact are already in place. It turns on a distinction between *profane* and *sacred*, a distinction which amounts to an original definition of religion. But Durkheim does not necessarily or essentially mean to reduce the latter to the status of a belief in personal supernatural beings. Everything thought to participate in the impersonal force that Melanesians call 'mana' is sacred, gods being only one of several possible modalities of such a participation. But everything in the order of the sacred is not therefore differentiated, and Durkheim does not situate religion and magic on the same plane. Religion represents a communion of faith of all the faithful, with magic therefore seeming to be its antithesis, since it knows no church, and is only defined in a haphazard way, by rules of convenience binding a magician and his client. Before returning to these distinctions and examining them more closely, it is worth remarking that Durkheim, in raising the question of the 'birth' of the sense of the sacred, is in fact posing the problem of its significance and function.

This is why psychologising interpretations, which invoke the influence of dreams or natural phenomena on individual minds in order to account for the formation of beliefs, seem to him not only to be inadequate, but also to have no bearing on their supposed object. Thus, for Durkheim, religion is essentially a social phenomenon, and he seeks to show by means of the 'simple' example of Australian totemism the relation between this phenomenon and the society in which it occurs. It is society's strength, and in this case the strength of the clan, which impresses primitive man. Totems, let alone the animals they represent, have no power in themselves and only become sacred because they symbolise clans. If one looks more closely one can therefore see that totemic representations refer to a double given: the clans they symbolise and the animals whose image they reproduce.

Durkheim accounts for the efficacy of this twofold representation by referring to the state of exaltation that characterises the periodic reunions of the group and which contrasts with the monotony of daily life, which is spent in more restricted social units. The notion of the sacred arises out of this effervescence and is identified with that of the clan symbolised by the totem; the unique or supreme god is merely one possible variant amongst a whole series of these modes of symbolisation, and it emerges, particularly in Australia, when totemism has not been developed by a single clan but by a whole tribe that has attained a certain awareness of its unity.

Lowie, in his *History of Ethnological Theory*, would seem to be fairly critical of Durkheim, more aware perhaps of the flimsiness of some of his hypotheses than of the originality of his overall project. In his critique, which is evolutionary in spirit, he points out that the clan is not the most ancient type of social unit, since it was 'preceded' by the family, and that Australian society is anyway not the simplest one known to us. There would therefore be no point, he argues, in seeking to learn something of 'the origins of religion' from it. Totemism,[10] he goes on to observe, is only one of several elements in the indigenous religion and there is no proof that the other aspects of religious life stem from it. I would note, in this respect, that Lévi-Strauss (in *Totemism*)[11] has addressed the same kind of criticism to Elkin and, more particularly, has shown that one cannot consider the various forms of 'totemism', i.e., its individual forms (an individual can acquire a totem, animal or vegetable, by inheritance or owing to the circumstances surrounding his conception or birth) and its social forms, as a single phenomenon. Lévi-Strauss observes that if Elkin had wanted to respect the unity of the Australian facts he ought properly to have abandoned totemism as a single and homogenous explanatory principle.

Such attempts to unify the apparently disparate aspects of phenomena postulated as essentially identical, and to discover a perspective from which

27

an underlying unity and a functional relation might be apprehended, are still clearly of interest, even in their contradictions and inadequacies. For each time an attempt of this sort has been made in anthropology, with varying degrees of success, it has been the starting-point for a series of more or less critical reflections. These in themselves represent a form of progress for research, and in any case lead to a refinement in theoretical formulation. I will cite, by way of example, some of these attempts, which are often of quite different theoretical inspiration. I have in mind Leach's[12] criticism of the distinction made by Meyer Fortes between unifiliation and complementary filiation, in favour of the two more comprehensive categories of incorporation and alliance, or Meillassoux's[13] and Terray's[14] application of the concept of mode of production to the study of 'primitive' societies. I shall refer again to these examples below, and shall feel all the freer in my mind for not being in complete agreement (as the reader will find out) with the conclusions reached.

As for Durkheim, we find that Lowie reproaches him for giving with one hand what he takes away with the other, and for appealing in the last analysis to a psychological notion (the state of exaltation) in order to account for belief in the sacred and its efficacy. Why, he goes on to observe, should one restrict the occurrence of this state to clan or tribal gatherings? Finally, Lowie asserts that, where problems of 'origin' are concerned, individuals have a real significance, in that deviations from the norm may become significant through the innovations that they bring, as one can see in the case of aboriginal millennial movements. He rebukes Durkheim for not taking sufficient account of the variable of the individual among 'primitive' peoples, and for speaking of them in *The Elementary Forms* in terms of moral and intellectual conformity, in terms of both a correspondence between conduct and thought and a confusion between individual and genetic type – all characteristics which would supposedly make them markedly different from 'more advanced societies'. Lowie observes that Boas and Thurnwald had already denounced this error, and makes the point that different versions of the same story can be collected within the same community. Yet this is hardly a conclusive example, for, on the one hand, since variations in a single story are not insubstantial, they comprise a system of transformations that cannot be accounted for merely in terms of the whim of individuals,[15] and, on the other hand, the problem of the place and expression of the individual in the social whole is not reducible to that of such-and-such an invention or variation either.

This point is important and will be found to have a central role in the most recent debates. The most sophisticated and dazzling version is to be found in those anti-State and anti-Oedipus philosophers (Baudrillard, Deleuze, Foucault, etc.) who credit primitives with a particular form of intersubjectivity, which exists prior to the pinning-down to oneself that the

28

Oedipal triangle represents. Dogon myths, African symbolism and masks would then all testify to the existence of a state in which the notion of the individual as consciousness 'apart' has neither meaning nor function. A subtler and more carefully argued version of this position is set out in Louis Dumont's work, particularly in his latest book, *From Mandeville to Marx*.[16] This approach clearly has several different repercussions. For if one invokes the moral and intellectual uniformity of primitive peoples one is both invoking the existence of a coherent body of 'representations' or categories permeating the different aspects of social and individual life, and implying that these are invariably used in the same way by each of the social factors. One is therefore postulating both an (intellectual) coherence and a (social) homogeneity. One is, in short, tending to relativise the difference between function and symbol in favour of symbol, and the various sorts of adherence to a totemic truth are then thought to constitute the mainspring of a symbolic efficacy that basically derives from a homogenous social order.

Louis Dumont, for example, begins with an intellectual and with a sociological distinction. The first is applied to the notion of 'the individual man' or of 'the individual', a notion which sometimes designates 'the *empirical* subject of speech, thought and will . . . as found in all societies', and sometimes 'the independent, autonomous, and thus (essentially) non-social *moral*, being, as found primarily in our modern ideology of man and society'. In other words, he opposes, in terms that neither language nor usage renders entirely unproblematic, the individual as empirical existent to the individual as value. It is, of course, the second that would be characteristic of modern ideology.

Dumont's second distinction refers to two types of society, 'holistic' and 'individualistic': 'According to the holistic conception, man's needs as such are ignored or subordinated, whilst according to the individualistic conception it is society's needs that are ignored or subordinated.' I ought to add that this distinction refers to 'higher' societies, and therefore to types and not to stages, even if our civilisation would seem to be the only one in which the individualistic type is historically attested. The hierarchy/equality contrast is one of the modalities of the holism/individualism opposition (the extreme case of a holistic society would be the kind of caste society that one finds in India),[17] and one can therefore see that, for Dumont, although he admits that hierarchy and individualism may in reality have different effects on the two sorts of society, the holism/hierarchy couple is still opposed to the individualism/egalitarianism couple. The fact of holism by no means implies egalitarianism, and vice versa, and neither mode is characteristic of any primitive society whatsoever.

It is thus clear that Louis Dumont's project contains positions that it would be of interest to compare, on the other hand, with those of structuralist theoreticians of the unconscious (where holistic or individualistic models would refer instead to what is implicit in societies), and, on the other hand, with those of the giant-killers engaged in fighting the accursed couple of Oedipus and the State. This project is also likely to short-circuit debates on the notions of culture and ideology (what is it in a 'model' that is expressed and what is it that is effective?), but it is enough for the time being to have given a context to the current debate on the reciprocal relations between individual and social reason.

I will now comment briefly on Lowie's overall 'objections' to Durkheim. I would note, first of all, that although some of the terms employed by Durkheim do call for the critical interventions that Lowie has made, the fundamental problem that he has raised would seem to me to be less that of the *origin* of religion than of its reason for existing or, better still, of its mode of existence. One could comment on Durkheim's work in the same way as one ought to comment on that of Rousseau: the problem, in Rousseau, is not one of knowing if historically there has ever been, through a real consensus, a social contract, but of noting that everything happens as if such a contract did exist and of wondering how far this hypothesis is a part of the implicit logic of a social system. Besides, the role of one or of several individuals in a particular religion, even in a millennial movement, interests me less than the whys and wherefores of that religion; and, beyond that, the whys and wherefores of religion in general; and beyond that, religion's relations with the sacred or with ideology in general. Durkheim's answers may be incomplete and unsatisfactory but they are made to fit the questions, which are, after all, general ones. The idea that primitive societies, more than others, 'run on ideology' (to take up one of Althusser's expressions), is still a startling one. It never ceases to attract anthropologists when they are investigating the two great problems, that of the difference between cultures and that of the functioning of symbols. Lowie's objections to Durkheim's definition of the clan as the simplest social form, and of totemism as the elementary religious form, are aimed at the evolutionist aspects of his thought, which are by no means the most important ones, and these objections are therefore of limited relevance. Even if clans and totems are not the first or simplest forms of religion the Durkheimian line of argument which is based on them, and which asserts the social essence of the sacred, is still an analysis of the first importance.

Let me turn now to the notion of 'representation'. If the sacred is a representation of the social, what is the social? What is the social, and what, for instance, is the clan before it is sacralised? In Durkheim's thought, as in that of many of his successors, the implicit hypothesis of a before or an after eliminates or blurs the real difficulties. Edgar Morin, in *Le Paradigme perdu*,[18] is effectively repeating Durkheim when, wishing to redefine sociology, he in his turn explains the efficacy of the social in terms of its sacralisation, without pausing to wonder what the social might really be before being sacralised – a question which would be meaningless if one had not set up a preliminary distinction between the profane and the sacred and distinguished clearly between the social and its representation. The notion of representation in the strict sense may be challenged, for it presupposes that, on the one hand, a represented social reality may be defined independently of its 'representation' (which, in my sense of the term, constitutes it) and that, on the other hand, the sacred may be wholly on the side of representation, guaranteeing the efficacy of the profane social order – and one is then entitled to ask what its own organisational principles are and where they originate.

An enquiry into the meaning and pertinence of the notion of representation thus leads one to enquire, in the second case, into the pertinence of the sacred/profane distinction, and likewise the religion/magic distinction. Lowie points out that with primitive peoples it is often difficult to distinguish between religion and magic, that certain functions, like that of the shaman, may be only very arbitrarily ranged within the second category, and that one cannot find the equivalent of the black mass in some types of society, even though Durkheim cites it in order to clarify his religion/magic opposition. It would seem to me more important to point out that, if one retains the categories of profane and sacred, one cannot find social activities that are strictly speaking outside the sacred, nor sacred activities that have no social applications or implications. It is, in short, the notion of profane activity that eludes analysis and represents something like the absolute limit to the thinkable; this makes Lowie's objection (why should profane festivals not generate a state of effervescence comparable with the state that religious festivals are held by Durkheim to generate?) self-defeating.

The problem is, therefore, one of knowing if, even in societies (for instance, ours) in which the profane/religious distinction is official and institutionalised, the category of the sacred does not by and large extend beyond that of the religious. Institutions, be they familial or political, are accepted, and one can enquire into the nature and modalities of this acceptance, but one cannot therefore treat it as a real and unproblematic fact through which one ought to think the social. Political anthropologists have for a long time been posing the problem of the relations between power and the sacred,[19] but beyond this one has to ask oneself what is the intellectual pivot of that alienation from institutions which is a corollary of all social existence.[20]

I would point out here, in passing, that our society's secular festivals (and from this point of view big sporting occasions, as reflected and retransmitted by the State apparatuses, are much more significant than the more marginal attempts) could well be considered the expression and the means (from my point of view these two terms would in these circumstances be synonymous) of an ideology without God and without faith but not without law, which, and this is the condition of all power, must be asserted as a necessity for each and for all. It seems to me obvious that there is ideology 'in general', as Althusser puts it, but I would also note how impossible it is to define a human individual who is not always already an individual in society, an individual who is caught by definition in relations of meaning and of power. The idea of this same ideology proceeding and working simply through the play of representations would seem to me, however, to be much more unlikely.

The general character of function (the integrative function of the sacred) is held by Durkheim to entail the specular character of symbols: a symbol's meaning is simply that part of the social order which it represents. This only explains how the social order *functions*, even if by way of the sacred representing it; the social order explains but may not itself be explained. Durkheim is less interested in specific combinations (i.e. 'cultures') than in the general correlations, which take the form of reflection, and this interest of his is subsequently developed by his successors, particularly by British anthropologists.[21] With them it takes the form of a distinction between religion as *expression* (of the rest of social life) and magic as *practice*; and this dichotomy often appears as one of the constraints within which functionalists work, when they have in fact to think about function. 'Marginal' practices and beliefs are then presented, not without contradiction, sometimes as a functional appendage to the system which is represented in religion (certain elders within a particular set of societies are, for instance, described as using their 'powers' to threaten younger people) and sometimes as an indirect condition of its dynamism and of its transformations (the young are then said, on account of the fear of sorcery that certain old people inspire in them, to be threatening them with secession).

Hubert and Mauss, in *Outline of a General Theory of Magic*,[22] conceive religion to be social and magic to be anti-social, but they place shamanism in this latter category, even though it is indisputably an important aspect of numerous religions. Moreover, witchcraft beliefs, which Hubert and Mauss also place alongside magic, correspond very exactly in numerous societies with an exact schema of social organisation. For the witches' power is supposed to be, on the one hand, acquired and inherited, and, on the other hand, exercised in very precisely defined spheres of social organisation. In this sense, these beliefs are, therefore, 'expressive' of the rest of the social organisation. There are, in short, many examples that serve to demonstrate the arbitrariness of any distinction between expressive and practical function, but it is symptomatic that an intellectual approach that still turns on the symbol–function axis and refuses to dissociate their opposed terms, will end up by appealing to a third category, and one that is in some sense infra-functional. This shows how necessary and yet how difficult it is to think both in terms of efficacy and in terms of history.

Symbol, function, culture

Malinowski[23] disregards the two other poles of the two other axes and pays almost exclusive attention to the culture–function relation. His relativism can take the form of a marked interest in the problems of individuals (in this he would be contrasted with Durkheim), and he contests the idea of a mechanical functioning of primitive laws; nevertheless, the individuality to which he refers is a wholly cultural one. This is clearly the case when, for instance, he tells us of the role of the father in the Trobriand Islands, a matrilineal society in which the authority relation between mother's brother and sister's son is much stressed. The influence that the father may exercise over his son in these circumstances, Malinowski tells us, depends on his personal authority. But the reader will note that the sort of individuality that is therefore at issue here refers to the relative positions occupied by the various partners in social life: *the* father in relation to *the* son, *the* uncle in relation to *the* nephew, etc. In none of his analyses does Malinowski disengage the notion of individuality from the socio-familial complex in which it is inscribed, and already defined as position and as role. Hence his recourse to the definite article (*the* father, *the* nephew), a hallowed ethnographic tradition that reproduces to a great extent the ideology that anthropologists ought to be accounting for, and suggests that all the fathers as fathers and all the uncles as uncles have the same problems and may be defined in the same way. Their individual personalities would then only affect things through the style in which solutions were tackled and answers given. Individuality, according to this viewpoint, is easily reduced to 'culture' (a Trobriand father is not an English or Tallensi father), and the meaning of symbols is thought to reside in intracultural functions.

Malinowski's 'functionalism' is also marked by a strong cultural relativism. I will not lay too much stress on the critique of the notion of need that could (quite properly) have been made here. It is quite clear, as Paul Mercier recalls, that in so far as he ties this term to a form of research where one does not simply ask 'how' but also asks 'why', Malinowski is vulnerable to criticism. It is also clear that the link posited between the general definition of peculiarly human needs (prolonged protection in infancy) and of 'derived' needs (the transmission of culture, communication), and the manner in which such needs are realised institutionally in different societies, is both obvious and paradoxical. It is obvious because to assert that every society functions is clearly, as Lévi-Strauss has observed, a truism, and whilst none would dispute that there is, for instance, a link between the necessity to take sustenance and the technical and social modalities by means of which food is produced and processed, to see in the former fact a sufficient cause for the latter procedures would be quite false as an explanatory deduction, and would clash with the reality of cultural relativism, which Malinowski does however affirm and reaffirm.

So this is the paradox: Malinowski's approach is in effect derived from his concern to reveal both the universality of the cultural process and the specificity of each integrated cultural ensemble. He is thus the first anthropologist to try, for what it is worth, to combine symbol with function without at the same time jettisoning culture. In this respect his virtues are great, and many of the attacks on his work would have benefited from his antagonists' acknowledging the intellectual wager which would seem to be at the root of his analyses. These attacks seem to be aimed sometimes at his 'provincialism', to use an expression of Lowie's and sometimes, on the contrary, at his eclecticism. These two objections are subtly undermined by Lowie when, after having reproached Malinowski for treating 'each culture as a closed system, except when its elements correspond to vital biological needs', he goes on to observe, with respect to the relations between marriage and sexual need, and between legal kinship and parental sentiments: 'I accept that all marriage forms have some relation to sexuality. But what I would like to know is why the Todas practise polyandry, the Bantus polygyny, and the Hopi monogamy; and that cannot be explained in terms of generic human tendencies, as Hocart has clearly recognised.' I would simply point out that the meaning of this 'why' is not very clear either, above all if one claims to answer it in culturalist terms.

Lowie does not stop there, but lists a certain number of questions that, ironically enough, retrace to a degree, albeit in an inverted form, Malinowski's own trajectory. It is culture in its entirety that concerns the anthropologist, he tells us; but this assertion does not, in itself, run counter to an approach in which one does in fact strive to break down the barriers between disciplines and to find in those among them that are concerned with the human pysche a general causal basis for particular cultural realities. We must, he adds, refer social traditions to the physical environments in which they occur, but this concern to anchor functionalism in a wider determinism does not in itself contradict the concern to define a culture as an integrated ensemble. As for this definition of culture, it certainly goes further than the simple assertion that 'several aspects of culture are closely interconnected and have a reciprocal influence on each other'. In that Boas asks that one study the technical or artistic productions of a people 'in an overall perspective' he is perhaps the first of the functionalists. Kroeber has studied the influence of dreams, chants and myths on the life of the Californian Indians, Cora Dubois has shown that the prestige attached to wealth is at the heart of Tolowa-Tutuni ideology, and Gayton, like Malinowski, and like many others since, has sought to demonstrate the social utility of witchcraft. But Malinowski goes further than this and, as Paul Mercier points out, his notion of 'culture', whilst it may respond to needs, is no longer composed of 'cultural features'

(features that circulate at the mercy of a diffusion whose scientific interest, and even whose reality, he denies), but of more complex ensembles, and of institutions orientated towards practice.

The most interesting intuition that functionalist theory provides is this: so long as one wishes to understand or, more exactly, to discern the co-herence of different types of social activity, it is impossible to sever them one from the other. This impossibility is the corollary of thinking the logic of the social. One cannot think about God or kinship on their own. Malinowski demonstrates this through the apparently 'economic' phenomenon of the *kula* (a circuit in the course of which special goods, according to procedures and a finality that are apparently not economic, are exchanged). To put it simply, he 'extracts' this example from the domain of cultural difference, in order to show how an activity that we consider to be economic may be analysed in terms that are not exclusively economic, and how exchange may be something other than market exchange. And if it is really true that the example of the *kula* brings to light social relations in which the limit be-tween the economic and the rest of social life is not clearly defined, we can ask in turn if the kind of solution in which one posits a continuity between what some Marxists call 'instances' ever exists, and therefore see in culturalism the theoretical limit to the usefulness of functionalism.

Malinowski tries by the same strategy to establish both the identity of each culture and the universalism of functions. There is a sense in which he presents a model which is almost the inverse of the one that structuralists will present, reducing the symbol to cultural relativism (if the Freudian analysis of repression is universally valid, in as much as there is always repression, the symbolic configurations that ensue are relative and irreducible cultural data), but universalising the primary functions, thereby outlining alongside a fairly mechanical materialism the sort of synthesis between meaning (univer-sal) and form (specific) that all anthropological theories of the mind tend to produce.[24] I could have criticised the excessively vague conception of primary functions or the excessively strict conception of functions of integration in evidence in Malinowski's work (Leach denounces the notion of integration as an observer's prejudice, and George Balandier has actually argued that all definitions of what a society is are 'problematic'). But such criticisms also testify, albeit indirectly or negatively, to the wide-ranging nature of a project that is never less than provocative. This is because it reverts again and again to one requirement: once one has analysed 'how' one should reformulate the question 'why'.

Of the authors whose work I have just surveyed, there is not one who actually ignores any of the four cardinal points of research (see diagram on p. 41). But anthropological navigation cannot be conducted simultaneously in all directions, and only its different wakes allow us to discern the entire circle that it describes. For Morgan it is above all a question of understanding the general evolution of society and the specific combinations of features that go to make up cultures. He thinks that it is possible to achieve this by defining each 'feature' as an index of evolution and by concerning himself only with the symbolic apparatus of a society in so far as it tells us something about that society's evolution. By treating the symbol–evolution relation in a particular way he relativises the polarity of the evolution–culture axis. Tylor tackles the same difficulties and also situates them on the evolution-culture axis, but it is function that he makes into an index of evolution, and it is the particular treatment of the function–evolution relation that has operative value for him. Durkheim's first priority is neither to discern the specificity of a particular culture nor to bring out the general laws of social evolution. He is the first to try to think of symbolic systems as possessing a particular efficacy which guarantees and conditions the functioning of social life. The debate that he inaugurates is basically situated on the symbol-function axis, whose terms are only opposed in order that their complementarity be understood. Malinowski in a sense makes the opposite choice, if only because he sets out from the intensive analysis of a particular society. Beyond the modes of integration particular to a society, which, because they are particular, can only be understood 'from inside', he searches for the expression of the more general functions that they fulfil. The debate instigated by Malinowski is therefore also situated on the symbol–function axis. He is the first anthropologist to have stressed the importance of Freud's contribution to anthropological research but he does not believe in the Oedipus complex, in as much as it is defined by a precise symbolic configuration; and for him this configuration is a function of each particular culture. It is thus the case that, in the matrilineal societies of eastern New Guinea, the mother's brother (who symbolises masculine potency more than the father does) would be more an object of respect, hate and envy than the father, whilst stray incestuous desires would be aimed more at the sister than at the mother. If the functions of repression are everywhere the same, the configurations are cultural, and Malinowski is committed above all to defining the relation between functions (general) and cultures (specific).

Culture, symbol

The connection between culture and symbol is the only one that would make it possible to close the circle, and this is still missing from my schema. That each culture possesses its own symbolic configurations is something that, in a certain sense, all anthropologists clearly have to admit. But to what extent are these particular configurations simply variations on the same central symbolic theme? To what extent have anthropologists tried to apprehend at once the universality of symbols and the specificity of culture? People have tried to do this from several different angles and within different theoretical perspectives, and a citation of these latter would introduce us to the most recent anthropological formulations. We can identify three different directions that this research has taken.

The first of these is culturalist, by which I do not mean American culturalism in the extremely relativistic form it assumes in Ruth Benedict's writing, although it is worth noting that even this hyper-relativism does itself become relativised. On the one hand, Benedict's work culminates in a distinction between several types or styles of cultures and revives Nietzsche's distinction between 'Dionysiac' and 'Apollonian' culture (in this respect she insists, as Malinowski does with respect to function, that behind the idea of a culture a universality is always posited); while, on the other hand, she asserts, both in her life and in her work, the need to better the lot of the human species and criticises the harmful aspects of certain cultures.[25] What I have in mind, rather, are the endeavours of the Griaule school, of Griaule himself and of those who have worked with him and after him, assembling the entire corpus of knowledge and mythical and symbolic constructions belonging to a sociologically and geographically defined 'culture'. This totality has to include the elements of 'profound knowledge' that, for Griaule and Dieterlen, belong only to a minority. The material gathered in Dogon country and in the surrounding areas[26] is in fact impressive. Neither Griaule, who died young, nor Dieterlen has ever thought to 'theorise' their empirical approach, but the sheer range and depth of their work has in itself generated new ideas. This is particularly true for French anthropological researchers, who tend to think of field-work as the tribute one has to pay (or the initiation one has to undergo) in order to accede to the title of theoretician. It goes without saying that their work represents a significant contribution to the comparative ethnography of the Sahel area, and on a scale that renders the notion of diffusion meaningful again. Their claim to reconstitute (or, ideally, to gather) a society's 'philosophy', means that, beyond any other considerations, a very particular domain becomes accessible to interpretation. The 'philosophy' of a society is in fact something that can be interpreted in its entirety from the point of view of symbolic meaning, without taking functional significance into consideration. It is something that lets itself be deciphered (that is, revealed gradually), and that only functions in the unchanging forms of gesture, object and rite, and as the fixed speech (*parole*) of myth. It is a reflection on man and society, on the birth and the order of the world, which is perpetuated from one generation to the next as an inaugural memory whose meaning only some have so far perceived, and in so doing have guaranteed that it is transmitted and that its expression is immortalised.

This conception of 'philosophy' (we shall see below the sorts of presupposition it obeys and the criticisms it gives rise to) justifies a systematic enquiry into the grand archetypes of mythical thought, which is as much as to say, of primitive thought, considered as inaugural of man and of the social. The

Freudian approach is clearly, in certain respects, marked by this tendency. In as much as he accepts the principle of ontogeny recapitulating phylogeny, Freud tends, on the one hand, to tie individual symbolism to the working of social repressions and, on the other, to define the elementary social institutions as being repetitions of humanity's primordial events, and the stages in the individual's development as being a recapitulation of stages in the development of humanity. He also establishes, in parallel to this, a strict correspondence between individual and social repression. So it is that for the Freud of *Totem and Taboo* the totemic feast is a repetition of the original parricide, and the Christian ritual a repetition of the totemic feast; but he also maintains that infantile animal phobias reproduce primitive totemism, and the latency period reproduces the ice age. Similarly, the Freud of *The Future of an Illusion* holds that the means man utilises to render the gods favourable to him have their prototype in the original experience he has, as a child, of his relation to his parents. One can clearly see that for Freud there is, from one society to the next, an identity of functions and an identity of symbols, and that the universality of symbols lays the foundation for that of culture. But one can also see that his 'transformationalism' oscillates between a static conception of a humanity whose languages would reproduce, universally and for all time, the inaugural event, and a more positivistic conception of progress, in which the idea of evolution, even if it is placed under the domination of the life and death drives, is not renounced.

My main interest here is the influence of Freudian analyses on current developments in anthropological theory. In so far as they are concerned with the social, symbolic and mythical expressions of incest and prohibition, these analyses cannot help but involve anthropologists. We shall thus see that, in France in particular, a whole group of researchers have taken their lead from materials of the sort that the Griaule school have gathered or from these materials themselves, and have attempted to discover, within the different cosmogonic themes (myths of twinship, of the founding hero, of incest) the fundamental expression of an archetypal relation to the *socius*. In that it is so exemplary the Dogon case may well give rise, as a recent issue of *L'Homme*[27] has shown, to quite technical anthropological debates concerning the links between alliance and descent, but in the background of this debate one can discern questions that are addressed to psychoanalysis. Psychoanalysis would thus reveal, at least for the structuralist Luc de Heusch, the deeper truth of a young man's aggressive behaviour towards his mother's brother in patrilineal systems. The 'more or less aggressive' privileges enjoyed by him would thus be 'the expression, real or symbolic of an unsatisfied claim (to the mother)', while his rights over the goods and wife of the mother's brother (among the Dogon or the Thonga) would be based on 'a symbolic reappropriation of the mother'. The allusions that are made in this sort of context to the 'psychoanalytic implications' of these observations or to the 'complementary interpretation' that psychoanalysis could add to them, are really circumlocutions, which leave intact the notion that ethnographic reality is based on analytic truth.

This convergence between an approach with analytic implications and a structuralist approach is not at all surprising, for both approaches tend to disclose, beyond cultural particularities, the identity of the human mind such as it is displayed in its cultural productions.

When Adler and Cartry[28] use these same materials to try and elicit a basic difference between types of symbolic expression and the modes that are operative in different societies, this identity is more or less relativised. It is therefore not surprising to find Deleuze and Guattari in *Anti-Oedipus* calling the Dogon to their rescue in order to discover in them the mark of a repression of 'intensive descent' (in which neither sex differences nor generation differences appear), which in principle has nothing to do with the Oedipus complex, but which is merely a later and displaced form of it. This expedient enables them to reintroduce a difference between the 'savage' and the 'civilised', a distinction which owes more to Nietzsche (for whom 'bad conscience' is historically situated) than to Freud (for whom the notion of 'original sin' is transmitted down the ages by means of hereditary predispositions). There is, by the same token, little in common between this distinction and that form of psychoanalytic relativism in which it is maintained that the Oedipus complex derives its efficacy from the fact that it binds desire to law, and in which it is no longer important to know if he who bars access to the mother or to the sister is or is not the real father.[29] The one thing that these various methodological approaches have in common is the fact that they all define symbols as 'expressive' either of the human psyche in general, in which case they are legible or decipherable (this is the universalist tendency of psychoanalysis), or of a particular state of humanity (this is the neo-evolutionist tendency, and it will become clear that it is more of a dichotomising tendency, reducing history to a before and an after with respect to the State).

Structuralists have similarly reduced culture to the symbolic, or, to put it differently, have favoured symbol over function. But such reductions are most characteristic of a form of 'geneticism' that psychoanalytically inspired interpretations in anthropology have always tended to produce. In this context history is thought to be nothing more than the manifestation, albeit transformed, of an inaugural event. Thus René Girard's *Violence and the Sacred*,[30] which is the most recent and in a sense the most spectacular expression of this tendency, has the unity of ritual as its central theme. Every ritual is taken to be a form, more or less transformed, of sacrifice, and every sacrifice a repetition of the act of violence that lays the foundation for the social order, an order which then strives to drive that violence out towards the outside, where it becomes an obsession and a threat. The high-flown idiom of modern 'para-anthropology' (in the sense in which one talks of a para-psychology) feeds off *motifs* of memory, repression and obsession. I would even go so far as to say that these comprise a set of themes marked and haunted by the anxieties of our epoch, and our interest in them stems from this. We ought in particular to be aware of the fact that, if *motifs* and frameworks recur, it is in the context of a history in which new stakes are becoming apparent. These exist in a context, that of the current situation in anthropology, and cannot be abstracted from it. The reader ought, moreover, to bear in mind that the outline I have given of an anthropological circle is merely to clarify things and however necessary is still provisional. It serves to situate my argument with respect to current discussion but also prevents me both from losing myself in fashionable debates and from adopting a Martian viewpoint (which is the one that all historians of anthropology have more or less had to adopt) and gazing coldly, like a god outside history, at the recurrent crises in human thought.

I have tried, using the pioneers of the subject as reference points, to discern the royal roads (cross-roads and blind alleys included) of anthropological debate. I will now pursue the opposite course and will show that there is no fundamental discrepancy between these paths and a number of current research preoccupations. Subsequently I will have to show how other anthropological objects and projects can be defined in terms of the same intellectual preoccupation.

By way of transition I would like to make two observations. I have emphasised how the structuralist approach, like those approaches which are analytically inspired or are para-anthropological, combines the themes of symbol and culture, relativising the latter in favour of the former. Again I should add that for Freud and for those inspired by him, if only to contest him, the reduction of culture to symbol is a feature of a debate whose point of departure may be situated on the symbol–function axis. For if, in many debates, symbols are only studied in terms of what they express, this expression itself refers to a general function of repression or of occultation. With Lévi-Strauss one has the impression that the symbol–function axis is more and more blurred until one can only discern the complementary terms of symbol and culture. The various forms of a myth, such as they appear in distinct but neighbouring cultures when transformed, in the end only set up a logic of relations which culminates in the myth referring just to itself and, in a way, to non-sense. 'The earth of mythology', Catherine Backès-Clément writes,[31] 'is round, and so much so that one does nothing but go round it in the same way; one repeats and one loses meaning in it.' She thus picks up one of Lévi-Strauss's phrases from *Mythologies* in order to show how his work has evolved since *Structural Anthropology*. In the latter, myth reflects the social system of alliance and kinship, albeit by inverting and obscuring it, whereas in the former, myth is considered to be a system so generally relativised that no real order is any longer reflected in it. From this point of view, for Lévi-Strauss, myth would remain, like music, 'the supreme mystery of the sciences of man'. We do after all know that Lévi-Straussian myth analysis depends on an analogy with the writing of music, its harmony (vertical and synchronic dimension) and melody (horizontal and diachronic dimension).

We thus find ourselves, through a movement that is itself circular, back at our starting-point. Sartre, in a recent interview,[32] tries to suggest how it might be that the music of a great composer, Bach or Beethoven, gives us the meaning of its own time and at the same time goes beyond that meaning: 'Beethoven's music is in fact the expression of the end of the eighteenth century and the beginning of the nineteenth century, but it is at the same time something massively larger, a kind of perspective on that time that one will always have from the outside . . . In short I would say that it is both the vision of the eighteenth century from the inside and also the vision of the eighteenth century from the outside.' It is fairly remarkable that, in order to express the secret of musical creation, Sartre appeals to the listener's feelings. For it is to us, as much as to the authors, that he assigns a double place (outside and inside) in order to apprehend a meaning that must at the same time be specific (cultural, historical) and universal. When anthropology manuals remind the ethnographer that it is necessary to practise both partic-ipant observation and distanciation, they are after all doing nothing more, if one sets aside the strictly methodological arguments, than recognising or positing the diversity of cultures and the universality of culture. The symbolic construction particular to each society should not be thought of as being an 'expression' peculiar to it (as seen from the inside) and a 'view of' this society (as seen from the outside), which would take us back to a specular inter-pretation of symbolism, but rather as being, a little like the musical work that Sartre was speaking of, its double meaning. It constructs its intimate and specific meaning, which is liable after all to become diversified and to find expression in multiple relations of significance and constraint, according to schemata homologous with those of other societies; this explains why no society, however different it appears, will be strictly speaking without mean-ing for the foreign observer.

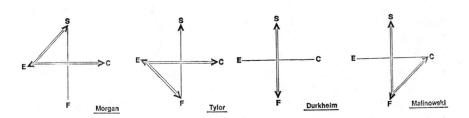

41

2

Some questions concerning the current state of anthropology

The philosopher's questions

Given the perspective adopted here, what can an expression like 'the current state of anthropology' mean? This question will be assessed in terms of the answers that may be given to it. First, there are certain dominant tendencies in anthropology, although one could qualify this assertion by pointing to the large number of by no means unimportant anthropologists who would refuse to align themselves with one of these, or indeed with any tendency whatsoever. But one can nevertheless maintain that their work does in part belong to one of these dominant tendencies, or that their contesting this simply serves to show that such tendencies do exist. My second answer in a sense reinforces the first one: there exists today, outside of anthropology in the orthodox sense, a general theoretical framework (or at least the bare bones of one) referring to anthropological materials and interpretations. Philosophers, in particular, put questions to anthropology or reformulate their own discipline in opposition to it (with all the ambiguity that this statement implies). These questions are addressed to structuralists, functionalists and Marxists and are clearly on the anthropological agenda. The problem that they rephrase or 'prioritise', as one says in political debates, are by no means unfamiliar to anthropologists. In this chapter I will therefore examine both the dominant theoretical configurations and the questions that tend to be put to them, the latter serving both to place and to undermine these configurations.

It is absolutely certain, however, that anthropology has not emerged unaltered from a century of history. It has been primarily an ethnology of colonised peoples and its founders could have had no idea of the situations that it has had to face and of the historical conjunctures in which it has been implicated. The crisis in anthropology, which takes in everything from moral anguish and intellectual doubt to political commitment, also provides an answer to the question asked at the start of the present chapter. I will study this crisis in the next chapter and will then proceed to ask what new sites and stakes there are, or could be, for anthropology.

The dominant theoretical alignments today are still concerned with the problems of symbol and function and with the associated problems of meaning. They feature, though in a different guise, in the work of a range of authors who speak both as anthropologists and as non-anthropologists but share a common interest in this set of problems. Thus, in *Anti-Oedipus*[1] Deleuze and Guattari assert that the important thing to know about any symbol is not what it means (admitting that, in this respect, it always refers us to the signified phallus), but 'what use it is' and, even more, 'how it works'. They do not themselves, however, remain faithful to this half-functionalist, half-phenomenological approach and when they consider a Dogon myth or a Gourmantché calabash to be expressive of a society's state they confine themselves to a narrowly exegetical interpretation. Castoriadis, in *L'Institution imaginaire de la société*,[2] criticises functionalism and Marxism on the one hand, and structuralism on the other, but his criticisms would not be out of place in the intellectual landscape that I have just surveyed. His main objection to functionalism (and also to Marxism, which in this respect he deems highly functional) lies in the fact that it posits a disjunction between a real order and a 'rational–functional' one. The latter is held to answer to the exigencies of the former, by means of institutions. God, reason, or the logic of history, are always, according to this perspective, the causes or aims of an unbroken chain of causes and effects, of ends and means.

Castoriadis acknowledges that Marx has a more finely drawn perspective than the one that informs Malinowski's functionalism. Thus, the latter asserts that 'in each type of civilisation, each custom, material object, idea and belief fulfils a vital function, has a task to perform and represents an indispensable part in the midst of a functioning whole'.[3] Marx, on the other hand, is aware of the exigencies of a social dynamic that mean that institutions do not adapt automatically to an evolution in technique but bring about delays through their own passivity and an evolution that proceeds in fits and starts. I would also note here that the Manchester school and the French 'dynamic' school, especially George Balandier, have paid particular attention to the manner in which these gaps and discontinuities emerge, and they may therefore be considered to be prolonging the functionalist tradition, albeit critically. Marx is, moreover, aware, Castoriadis reminds us, of the autonomisation of the institution as a source of alienation, but he has 'a functional view of alienation itself'. What is still obscure, as much in the Marxist as in the functionalist perspective, is the reality criterion affecting the needs (in Marx 'the needs of the exploiting class to dominate') which provide the foundation for the appearance of, and explanation of the rest, i.e., of institutions. For whilst Castoriadis quite clearly holds that institutions fulfil a vital function, without which society's existence would be inconceivable, it is still the case that institutions are not reducible to this role and this role does not itself render them perfectly comprehensible. All institutions are not functional and in certain societies there are functions that could be fulfilled by them and, taking into account the level of historical development, are not.

But if it is therefore impossible to reduce institutions to their functionality, it is equally impossible to reduce them to the status of a pure symbolic network, and Castoriadis does not subsume under the category of symbol what he excludes from that of function. His basic objection to Lévi-Strauss resides in a twofold assertion: first, he maintains that there is a meaning which can never be given totally independently of signs, but which is something other than an opposition between signs; and second, that it is a capitulation to the century's Utopianism, which tends to eliminate both meaning and man, to make meaning out to be nothing other than the result of a combination of signs. One clearly cannot deny that the institutions' symbolic network must refer to something other than symbolism if it cannot be reduced to the functions that it would supposedly fulfil. In a series of texts written in 1964 and 1965[4] Castoriadis commented on the development of Lévi-Strauss's thought, relying particularly on his answer to Paul Ricoeur in *Esprit*, November 1963 ('You claim that *The Savage Mind* opts for syntax as against semantics; for me there is no such choice . . . meaning always arises from the combination of elements that are not in themselves signifying') and on a now famous passage from *The Raw and the Cooked* (1964): 'I claim to show not how men think in myths but how myths are able to think through men's minds without their knowing it. And . . . it would perhaps be appropriate to go still further and disregard the human subject altogether, in order to see how one could, in a certain sense, consider myths as thinking *amongst themselves*.'[5]

Castoriadis holds that Lévi-Strauss evades three crucial questions, the first of which is the question of content, of reference to the signified. Taking up Lévi-Strauss's own phrase, which suggests that certain animal species are invested with totemic qualities because they are 'good to think with', Castoriadis wonders why one set of species rather than another should be chosen for this purpose, and why one couple of oppositions rather than another should be constituted. The second question bears on the requirement that there be meaning. Contrary to what pure structuralism proposes, one could argue that the combination of signs is a consequence of meaning and that there would be no structuralist musicologists if there had not first been a creator and musician to choose sign oppositions as a function of meaning. One should not confuse the conditions necessary for the reading of a work with those that are necessary for its existence. The third question bears on the why and wherefore of an institution's autonomisation: 'How and why does an institutional structure, no sooner installed, become a factor to which a society's actual life is subordinated and as if enslaved?' This question also raises the problem of the institution's alienation from the very people who dominate and control it.

The philosopher's questions

It is clear that all of these questions that are addressed to functionalism and structuralism are not dissimilar from the circular chain of reasons and interpretations that I have tried to reconstitute above. Having raised these questions, Castoriadis actually re-examines the symbol–culture relation, wondering if the social imaginary might not be reducible to the individual imaginary, and if reductions of the sort that Freud had attempted in the case of religion might not offer a complete explanation. He concludes, how-ever, by answering No, and by suggesting that it is on the contrary perhaps the individual unconscious that is the result of the social imaginary. I will return to these terms and to this suggestion below, but deem it adequate for the time being to have identified the range of questions formulated by Castoriadis.

Let us now consider the work of Pierre Bourdieu, an author who speaks 'from the inside' and whose questions are addressed more particularly to structuralism. In a very astute article,[6] he enquires whether every analysis of religion in terms of symbolic significance is not incompatible with the study of functions and of the role that it plays with respect to social life's non-religious aspects. He is thus able to contrast a Durkheim–Lévi-Strauss line of descent with a Marx–Weber one, with the former perspective being possible only at the price of a 'radical doubt' as to the social function of religion, and *a fortiori* as to the role that it can play as an instrument by means of which some dominate others. On the other hand, only Weber may be said to have resolved the problem, which Marxism has merely raised, by showing how a body of specialists guarantees ideological production in diverse societies. Three observations could be made here.

First, it is important to make it clear that religion does not fall from the sky and that one can identify actors who produce it, and its different modali-ties; but this observation does not in itself resolve the problem of the relation of the religious sector to the rest of social life, any more than it resolves that of the 'production' of non-religious social institutions. The problem of the institution's efficacy, or of its alienation (to use Castoriadis's language), is also unresolved. Second, there is doubtless some methodological value in asserting that one cannot at the same time treat religion as expression and as a system of knowledge, and define it as a system that has efficacy in the social sense, but one does not thereby explain why it is effective, and perhaps this is simply because there has been no attempt to envisage what a properly symbolic efficacy might be. Third, by suggesting that the study of the economic and social functions of religious systems can, in the case of 'less differentiated societies', be usefully shelved in favour of apprehending their structural aspects, Pierre Bourdieu[7] condemns these societies to a startlingly separate destiny. For it is even more difficult in these societies to distinguish what would and would not be religious, since relations with men and with things bring into play in a much clearer way than elsewhere the full range of sym-bolic systems.

In another text, *Outline of a Theory of Practice*,[8] Bourdieu criticises structuralism from another angle. He points out that when one is studying phenomena that are constituted across time, a synchronic apprehension of the meaning with which the practice is invested becomes impossible; one can only give a full account of the significance of the gift when the return gift has occurred, which, in answering the gift, gives it both its measure and its meaning. The best proof of this lies in the fact that the return gift constitutes by itself a provocation that calls for a response, the latter having to be both a function of the gift and of the return gift. Anthropological literature and experience provide us with a host of examples of social phenomena whose meaning is always to a large extent retrospective. It is obvious in the case of phenomena of economic display of the *potlatch* type, which entail struggles for influence and prestige whose meaning may be deferred, in as much as the partners confronting each other delay the moment of reckoning. But it is true also (and from this point on, Bourdieu's analysis may be extended) of other phenomena, whose diachronic dimension is less immediately apparent but which, if one is to preserve any chance of interpreting them, must not be ignored. This is not only because they are phenomena which endure, but also and above all because they are in some respects reconstituted and redefined at each stage in their development.

If witchcraft in black Africa really does constitute a practice and not just a system of beliefs, it is not because some Africans are endowed with a special talent for ubiquity or for exerting a psychic influence on others, but because, as a function and effect of these sorts of belief, closely tied as they are to an exact definition of social hierarchy and lineage logic, modes of behaviour are possible which, setting up a relation of force, only derive their meaning from the reception they are given and from the response or counter-attacks that ensue. The actual meaning of the phenomenon, in its most general sense, therefore stems from the possibility of defining the virtual logic of the sequences that constitute it and not only or essentially from the 'harmonic' dimension of each of its moments. Harking back to the musical metaphor used by Lévi-Strauss in his analysis of 'mytho-logics' it has to be said that, where practices are concerned, the 'melodic' dimension, in as much as it is not defined by the contingent addition of elements analogous to 'mythemes' but is, on the contrary, subordinated to the constraints which make up the social order, is the essential and in the last analysis the only pertinent one. A simple example may help to illuminate this.

Suppose that a number of deaths occur in an African village, inhabited by several lineages; suspicion will then be aroused, for every event, and above all if it is repeated, demands to be interpreted. But this interpretation is not random. The identity of the dead and knowledge of their familial problems, and of the problems of others, will determine the direction that diagnosis will take. The fundamental principle that all the different conceivable types of interpretation will have in common is that all physical or physiological disorder refers to a social disorder, not in the sense that one reflects the other (this is a possible 'reading' but it will only provide insight into the coherence of each moment in the process – vomiting or spitting blood is for instance associated with a woman's adultery, a gradual weakening with a witchcraft attack), but in the sense that both of them refer to the same interpretational grid and contribute to the gradual and problematical definition of a logic of practice. Not just anyone will be in a state to set up a particular type of interpretation. This is not only because there are specialists in interpretation, but above all because, taking into account the identity of those presumed to be responsible for the deaths that have occurred, and the respective positions of (social) strength of accusers and accused, the 'trial' (which is both a process and an accusation) will or will not proceed, and if it does, it will unfold in conditions that vary with the reactions of the parties concerned. It is the whole social order that may be read in a 'trial' of this sort, whether it turns on a settling of accounts within the lineage or on a quarrel between allied lineages, but its anthropological interest derives less from this possible transcription of the social order than from the modalities of its inscription, which go to make up the order itself. It is all the possibilities of practice that define the necessity of order.

But there is also an order of possibilities, for not every scenario may be thought of as occurring. Bourdieu specifies here that these possibilities may not be counted and that actual practices are not the result of a choice between a fixed number of formulae. Like Dan Sperber in *Rethinking Symbolism*,[9] he is concerned rather with the degree of openness of a particular culture's cognitive field, as understood in Chomskyan terms. Sperber puts it like this: 'The schema that "brings order to action" is neither a "plan" consciously established in advance that one would simply put into practice . . . nor is it an "unconscious" that would mechanically direct action', and 'No signification in universal myths, but, when all is said and done, a universal focalisation, a field of cultural and of individual allusions.' And as Chomsky himself puts it: 'A person who knows a language has represented in his brain some very abstract system of rules that determine by free iteration an infinity of sound–meaning correspondence.'[10]

For the time being we should simply bear in mind that this openness of practice to the future, an openness which lends or reascribes a meaning to it, is undoubtedly a characteristic of ritual activity in general; the carrying out of a ritual act entails a risk, for the one who orders that it be done and for the one who executes it, in so far as its efficacy must itself be practical if it is to exist as symbolic. The rain-master who fails to dispel a drought or the head of a kingdom who fails to conquer his enemies does not do so with impunity, for the meaning of a rite depends in the last analysis on being sanctioned by the event which does itself transcend the symbol/function

47

alternative. Obviously, the rite's meaning may not be reduced to the problem of the successful fulfilment or not of its explicit aim, but it does indeed depend on it, and may far less happily be reduced to the reading that may (or may not) be given of its different formal moments. It is clearly fairly noteworthy that Lévi-Strauss is more interested in myths than in rites, and in a reading of meaning which may, in the long run, reveal only the original arbitrariness of non-sense (of the signifier) rather than revealing the intellectual structures of practice. Can there strictly speaking be a science of change or, at any rate, a science of practice? This question brings us to a cross-roads at which various incompatible forms of research meet. It is both the point of their divergence and also the sole thing they have in common. If we return to it again and again it is because it provides a yardstick with which to take the measure of an irreversible disagreement, and because it enables us to imagine, if not to grasp, the possibility of another dimension and another conceptual space.

The enquiries whose basic nature I have just summarised may be said both to specify and to undermine the anthropological achievements of the last thirty years. This placing in question/placing in context would seem to rest on two principles that it would be both interesting and necessary to isolate. First, it upholds the central aspirations of anthropology. It is the easiest thing in the world to deride all such totalising ambitions, and one might just as well denounce, in the name of a 'down to earth' common sense that has every chance of hitting its target (especially since its criticisms often turn out to be justified), the speculative and risky nature of all intellectual constructions. English anthropologists will sometimes ask such and such a representative of the French research tradition: 'What evidence do you have?' They are right to do so, in as much as they are alluding to the sort of intellectual short circuit which is one of our temptations and which has led some of our great predecessors to reconstruct an African society's system of thought without really being interested either in their kinship system or in their economic system, or some of our contemporaries to prefer theorising from others' research materials and to refuse to 'surrender' their own, no doubt fearing that they have not elaborated them sufficiently and that they will have to surrender them to the intelligent rereading of more patient and astute colleagues.[11] But risk is an intellectual virtue too, and the distinction between description and interpretation can easily turn into the most artificial and fallacious of interpretations. British anthropologists are as aware of this as anyone, as is demonstrated by the fact that the most speculative of French theoreticians[12] always prefer to cite the great names of British anthropology, past and present, because of the theoretical arguments they have advanced. The British[13] and Americans[14] do increasingly feel and express the need for an anthropology which, as I shall show below, is not limited in its theoretical object to one geographical, cultural and temporal framework.[15]

Structuralist, functionalist and Marxist ambitions are still totalising ones, and their various projects have in common the fact of arriving, by different paths, at a placing in question or a refinement – and this is the second of the two principles just mentioned – of the notion of 'representation'. Even when neither of these words is uttered, it is invariably around the notions of rationality and representation that current theorists are refining their own positions (and amongst these I would include those who are interested first and foremost in the constitution and reproduction of social relations of reproduction). These notions are likewise at the heart of the questions addressed to anthropology by writers like Deleuze and Guattari, for whom social and symbolic configurations must be something other than the straightforward representation of a supposedly universal psychic symbolism. For Castoriadis the real/rational-functional disjunction has no meaning, and he tries to analyse, beyond the arbitrary complications of symbolism, the laws of functioning of a social imaginary in which neither social practice nor institutions are dissociated from their representation. Bourdieu, on the other hand, treats the logic of practice in such a way that there is no necessity for the notion of model to be associated with that of synchrony.

It is fairly remarkable that with all these authors one can observe more or less clearly emerging the project of considering the *efficacy* of symbolic practices and of bringing out the necessarily symbolic part of any socially constituted reality. It is fairly remarkable too that they are all more or less explicitly aware of the need to construct a logic of actual practices, of structures of diachrony and of schemata. The enquiry into function and structure therefore culminates in the posing of new questions and sometimes in the proposing of new terms. To raise questions as to the *efficacy* of symbols is to have in mind not so much their *function* as the mechanism by means of which they intervene; and to provide a theory of practice is not merely to understand the unconscious *structure* of the representations which govern it, but also to reveal the schemata constitutive of every representation, and thereby actually to alter the meaning of the term 'representation'. Having said this, I would add that these new questions and outlines have been rendered possible only through the development of modes of thought that are well and truly structuralist, functionalist and subsequently Marxist.

I will therefore not try to give here an exhaustive or systematic account of these modes of thought but to recall some of the main lines of argument, as exemplified by particular authors and works. There is no authorised representative of structuralism apart from its founder, Claude Lévi-Strauss,[16] in France or anywhere else. Functionalism informs the work of numerous anthropologists, sometimes in a manner that is not at all conscious, but in the work of an author as rich in insight as Victor Turner it has developed into a neo-functionalism critical of studies more systematically devoted to the problem of symbolic efficacy, and this development seems well suited to reveal this method's value, its limits and the sense in which it can be superceded. If, finally, the sometimes conflicting approaches of Marxist[17] anthropology characterise a certain number of French authors, whose work should be cited if one is to grasp the innovatory character of this 'strand', Maurice Godelier is clearly the person who has hitherto sought most explicitly to define what, when considered in relation to the approaches of structuralism and functionalism, a Marxist approach ought to be.

Structuralism tackles the question of the compatibility of meaning and structure, and more particularly, investigates that twilight zone where meaning fades into non-meaning. Functionalism, in the form in which it has been gradually elaborated by Turner, distinguishes between a structural level in society (in the empirical sense of the term structure, the sense that Radcliffe-Brown has given it) and an infrastructural level which is marginal (in the sense of an 'aside' or a 'within' of structure), and through which society, paradoxically enough, regains and reproduces its cohesion. This functionalism raises implicitly the question of infrasymbolic efficacy. Marxism, whose 'functionalist' aspects are quite properly emphasised by Castoriadis, has to cope with the difficulties raised by the language of instances. This language encourages the notion that, on the one hand, superstructures are sites for the expression of contradictions that are produced and resolved somewhere else (and it is therefore liable to the same criticisms as the most specular of functionalisms), and that, on the other hand, every social formation is a combination of modes of production (thus giving rise to the suspicion that it is prey to a kind of intellectual ethnocentrism, projecting on to all societies categories tied to the analysis of nineteenth-century European societies). Implicitly, through its own inadequacies, or explicitly, through the criticism that some Marxist anthropologists make of their own intellectual instruments, Marxism raises the question of the functionalism of instances and of structural efficacy.

Meaning, non-meaning and structure: Claude Lévi-Strauss

Quite apart from the wealth of insights that it contains, Lévi-Strauss's work seems to me to have a pivotal role in relation to two of anthropology's most urgent preoccupations. He tries very explicitly to place his work in relation to the irreducible polarities that the axes of classical anthropological research involve, whilst also assigning the same (symbolic) status to the different modalities of social organisation. He thus provides himself with the means of building an intellectually rigorous theory, and the most constructive of his critics are doubtless indebted to him for it.

Lévi-Strauss has a definite tendency to qualify the opposition between the supposed universality of evolution and the specificity of cultures, on the one hand, and the supposed universality of symbolism on the other.

But he is not unfamiliar with two problems that, far from being resolved by his theory, have often been shown to haunt it; these are the problems of function and history.

Evolution and culture are two terms that ought, properly speaking, to be mutually exclusive. Lévi-Strauss expresses this as clearly as anyone in some lines from 'Race and History':[18] 'Caught between the double temptation to condemn experiences which give him an emotional shock and to deny differences which he cannot understand intellectually, modern man gave free rein to a hundred philosophical and sociological speculations in order to establish futile compromises between these contradictory poles and to account for the diversity of cultures, while seeking to suppress that which seems to him scandalous and shocking.' But this compromise can in fact lead to only one recipe, and one that Lévi-Strauss terms *false evolutionism*, both because it has nothing to do, from the point of view of scientific rigour, with Darwin's biological evolutionism,[19] and because it suppresses the diversity of cultures whilst pretending to acknowledge it: 'For if one treats the different states of human societies, both ancient and distant, as *stages* or *steps* of a single development which, starting from the same point, must then all converge toward the same goal, it is quite evident that diversity is only apparent.' Against an evolutionism that reduces cultural specificities, Lévi-Strauss proposes the idea of a more diversified progress.

He first observes that, with advances in prehistory and archaeology, we tend more and more to accept that different forms of civilisation could have existed and been spread out in space instead of being staggered in time. 'Progress' could thus have proceeded by 'leaps' or 'bounds', or as biologists would say, by 'mutations', without its being the case that human history should everywhere find expression in an accumulation of gains: 'It is only from time to time that history is cumulative, i.e., that the numbers can be added up to form a favourable combination.' At this point Lévi-Strauss's thought veers towards a sort of cultural relativism: cumulative history, he tells us, is not the privilege of one civilisation or of one historical period, but it is often difficult for us to perceive it when it tallies with a culture which develops values that are foreign both to our own, and to the civilisation through which we observe the other. Just as old people can hardly find any meaning in a historical period in which they are no longer actively engaged, or just as, for a traveller in a train, 'the speed and length of other trains vary according as to whether they are moving in the same or in opposite directions', so too would we find ourselves, given the manner in which western civilisation has devoted itself for two or three centuries to increasing the quantity of energy available per head of population, incapable of describing the history of others from any other point of view. And yet, if one were to adopt other criteria, other civilisations would bear off the prize: the Eskimo and Bedu for their adaptation to hostile geographical environments, Islam for its theory of solidarity between the various forms of human life, and the East and Far East for knowledge of the body and of the relations between physical and moral being.

This relativism does nevertheless founder on the overwhelming evidence that there is for the universalisation of western civilisation; the fact that we do not yet know the result of the phenomena in progress (what syncretisms or what backlash are we heading for?), and the fact that allegiance to the western way of life is, as Lévi-Strauss quite rightly notes, the result of an unequal balance of forces, in no way undermines this evidence. To account for it and thereby to weaken its hold, Lévi-Strauss advances three kinds of complementary reflections. He points out first that no invention is due to chance, that observation, reflection and experimentation have been necessary across the ages, and that anyone who posits an opposition between periods or states of civilisation during which technology fell from the sky (fire being the result of a chance bolt of lightning, pottery the result of forgetting a pellet of clay beside the fire) and periods of systematic reflection and of inspired intuitions, is totally unaware 'of the complexity and diversity of operations implied in the most elementary techniques'. However, chance does have a role to play, and, more specifically, Lévi-Strauss notes that, twice in its history, humanity has accumulated a certain number of inventions 'pointing in the same direction' within a fairly short lapse of time. This meant that 'highly technical syntheses', themselves entailing a certain number of 'chain reactions', could occur. These two occasions were the Neolithic Revolution and the Industrial Revolution. Give or take one or two hundred years, the Neolithic Revolutions were unleashed almost simultaneously in the world, and we know how rapid the spread of the Industrial Revolution has been: 'if, as is likely, it is to spread to the whole of the inhabited globe, each culture will introduce so many particular contributions that the historian of the distant future will rightly hold as futile the question of knowing who, within one or two centuries, may claim to have been the first.'

The third observation is something more than an observation, bearing as it does on the theme of collaboration between cultures and on that of the double meaning of progress, a theme which constitutes the last movement of 'Race and History'. The most cumulative historical forms, its author notes, have never occurred in isolated cultures, but in those that combine 'voluntarily or involuntarily, their respective games', which can thus more easily realise the sorts of long series favourable to the syntheses invoked above. The greater the differential gaps between the cultures facing each other, the greater the range of possibilities, and the more chances there would be for invention and integration. Lévi-Strauss is thus able to contrast the example of Europe at the beginning of the Renaissance, where Greek, Roman, Germanic and Anglo-Saxon traditions converged with Arabic and Chinese influences, thus making it the product 'of a differentiation several millennia old', with that of America at the same epoch. Cultural contacts were doubt-less as numerous there but, because settlement was more recent, the overall cultural picture was more homogenous, so that, in spite of their superiority in other respects, Pre-Columbian civilisations turned out to be full of 'lacu-nae'. Their lack of flexibility, and consequently of diversity, may well account for their collapse before a handful of conquerors: 'The deep cause for it may be sought in the fact that the American cultural "coalition" was established between partners who differed less among themselves than did those of the Old World.'

One can thus see how ambiguous the notion of progress is if one identifies it with the world-wide extension of civilisation or of culture. In order for a world-wide civilisation to remain creative it also has to remain relative, a 'coalition' of different cultures; there is therefore, in the last analysis, a contradiction between a sharing of resources that produces a gradual hom-ogenisation and that diversity which is so necessary for progress. Lévi-Strauss notes in this respect that the great revolutions, Neolithic and industrial, are accompanied by social diversification and differentiation. He diverges here from Marxism in suggesting that the link between technological revolu-tion and social transformation is one not of causality but of functional corre-lation, and that, with the expansion of capitalism in the nineteenth century, it is imperialism and colonialism that have introduced the element necessary for diversification and renewal.

I am inclined to think that this argument, in spite of its brilliant and pro-ductive analyses, raises two problems; first, the status that Lévi-Strauss gives to history and to the historicity of human societies, and second, the place that may be given to the universal notion of the unconscious in an approach which so clearly favours the irreducibility of cultures and the importance of contacts and of diffusion.

When reproached for seeking to disregard history, Lévi-Strauss has often objected, but we should weigh our words carefully here. I would be quite prepared to argue that Lévi-Strauss, in so far as he is not interested in re-lations of force internal to a society or in relations of domination between societies, disregards history. Here too he could object, and quote the very texts that I have just summarised, texts in which class relations on the one hand and imperialist social relations (of domination) on the other are pre-sented as logically linked to technological revolutions. But this 'functional' connection is presented only as the necessary condition for the enrichment of the societies in which it appears. In the case of men, humanity and cultures, it is as if, after a few random events and encounters, history were quite literally to marry into a societal game in which the partners' identity matters less than the series of throws of the dice, none of which, in spite of some recurrences and the overall development of the game, ever (as Mallarmé put it) abolishes chance. History must, in short, like structure, be without a subject, or have no other subject than those ideal entities (civilisations, cultures, societies) which may be apprehended as just so many intellectual objects existing outside of praxis.

The fact that synchrony is favoured over diachrony implies that relations of domination are interesting only in so far as they allow a society to order its diversity and an observer to understand such an order; that they do, in short, have only an indirect and synchronic intellectual finality. History is thus nothing but 'the reconstitution of a "past", which is simply considered as "distant", and not the apprehension of a temporality, of a properly historical movement that, in its very quality as movement, would create its own sense of meaning'.[20] When Jean Pouillon thus discusses the Lévi-Straussian conception of history, his comparison between a game of chess (that Ferdinand de Saussure had used to illustrate the independence of the synchronic dimension in linguistics, 'that any given position has the singular property of being divorced from those preceding it') and a game of bridge (in which knowledge of the preceding tricks is indispensable for the understanding– or execution – of the end of the game) is perfectly admissible. 'The order of bridge', Pouillon writes, 'is a diachronic one, whereas that of chess is synchronic.' But one ought also to point out that this distinction between two modalities of anaylsis is valid for a number of institutions and social practices (consider, in this respect, the practices that Bourdieu analyses), and that it is therefore applicable to the problem of praxis in general, and not only to the history of societies. Furthermore, one cannot conceive it except in terms of categories or historical actors caught up in a history that is irreducible to the half-contingent, half-necessary play of cultural inventions and precipitates.

At this point various anthropological approaches again falter and appear self-defeating: if history has a meaning, apprehension of the given states of a society may perhaps not contradict the search for this meaning, but it is clearly not enough to confine oneself to this task, and if history has no meaning there is no point in unmasking the 'ambiguities' of the idea of progress, for one cannot, strictly speaking, conceive of progress at all. Lévi-Strauss is perhaps never so much himself or never follows his own natural bent so far as when, in *Tristes Tropiques*,[21] as Pouillon points out, he attributes only one problem to men, that of making a society transparent to itself. This endeavour can only be repeated and therefore dissipated, the installation of the reign of culture being identified once and for all with 'the indefinable grandeur of beginnings', and the ethnographer's task then lies in understanding a society in order to reveal 'the deformed but recognisable structure which refers to the essence of its beginning' and 'to imagine the ideal conditions which could have maintained it indefinitely at its first beginnings' (Pouillon). One can clearly perceive a profound link here between the structuralist approach and the different kinds of 'geneticist' approach, whether psychoanalytic in inspiration or not, for which history, beneath the apparent complexity of events, is never anything else but the repetition of the act that founds the original order.

One can also perceive here the importance of a category which is linked to this very particular conception of history, but which, though essential to structural analysis, is never allowed exactly the same weight or status in Lévi-Strauss's work. I refer here to the category 'the unconscious'. This term is first understood in relation to the 'universal laws which regulate the unconscious activities of the mind',[22] laws whose existence guarantees the possibility of a comprehension or of a communication between different cultures, and even, in the last analysis, between subjectivities dependent on particular cultures. In his 'Introduction à l'œuvre de Marcel Mauss' Lévi-Strauss defines the unconscious very precisely. It is the domain in which objective and subjective meet, and is 'the middle term between self and other'. Jean Pouillon[23] is right to point out here that the unconscious structure to which one would then have access is common to various cultures and that this identity in no way contradicts the diversity of cultures; that, in short, it does not relativise anything, whereas an analogical conception of cultures would lead one to relativise their differences at the same level as they were observed. The identity of cultures is thus taken to be situated elsewhere than in their diversity.

It is not altogether certain, having said this, that Lévi-Strauss's category of the unconscious is defined in a rigorously homogenous fashion throughout his own work. I will simply indicate three different sorts of emphasis. In *The Elementary Structures of Kinship*[24] the unconscious refers to the necessities of social organisation (to the necessity of exchange) and expresses itself in a symbolic thought so redolent with meaning that the meaning/function distinction is absolutely displaced. The Bororo myth in *Tristes Tropiques* conceals or 'disguises' the reality of social relations, and the unconscious therefore has as its function to obscure things in a certain way. In *Mythologies*, however, the internal logic of myths and of their system of transformation is studied for its own sake and does not refer to any real order other than that of the mythical figures who people the narrative (animals, stars, etc.). It therefore follows that the notion of the unconscious does itself, in failing to correspond to any subject whatsoever (through which consciousness might, either as complement or as contrast, be defined), lose all meaning.

The incest prohibition is a universal institution for Lévi-Strauss and it is expressed by positive rules, of which all societies, or rather most of those who compose such societies, are perfectly conscious. They are moreover capable, should the occasion arise, of formulating some of their functions or consequences; but these rules (as expressed in dual organisation, for instance) have to be understood in terms of 'certain fundamental structures of the human mind' that Lévi-Strauss enumerates: 'The exigency of the rule as a rule; the notion of reciprocity regarded as the most immediate form of integrating the opposition between the self and others; and finally the synthetic nature of the gift, i.e., that the agreed transfer of a valuable from one individual to another makes these individuals into partners and adds a new quality to the value transferred.'[25] It is the action of these structures that explains why it is that, in the last analysis, the exchange of women can be analysed as linguistic exchange, and that exogamy and language may be considered to have the same communicatory function. But Lévi-Strauss defines other 'structures', which are, strictly speaking, elementary structures of kinship, and which are the equivalent of the general model that the observer may construct by means of the rules that are actually applied in concrete societies:

> We have thus established that superficially complicated and arbitrary rules may be reduced to a small number. There are only three possible elementary kinship structures;[26] these three structures are constructed by means of two forms of exchange; and these two forms of exchange themselves depend upon a single differential characteristic, namely the harmonic or disharmonic character of the system considered. Ultimately, the whole imposing apparatus of prescriptions and prohibitions could be reconstructed *a priori* from one question and one alone: in the society concerned, what is the relationship between the rule of residence and the rule of descent? Every disharmonic regime leads to restricted exchange, just as every harmonic regime announces generalised exchange.[27]

The elementary structures refer less here to the unconscious of societies than to the consciousness of their observer, but they are at the same time the transcription of fundamental structures of the human mind, such as one sees at work in symbolic forms other than kinship systems. They are, nevertheless, specific, in as much as they express, for Lévi-Strauss, a fundamental necessity, a necessity of meaning and function which is the actual essence of social necessity: for society to be possible and thinkable women have to be considered as signs.

What other symbolic manifestations are there? The basic one in Lévi-Strauss's work, as represented by the four volumes of *Mythologies*, is that of myth. This form is tied to a given place and time, but is subject to systematic transformations within a determinate cultural area. Lévi-Strauss had already embarked upon the study of myth in other parts of his work, and I will refer here to the previously quoted article by Catherine Backès-Clément, which shows quite clearly how his analyses evolved from *Tristes Tropiques* to *Mythologies*.

Bororo myth describes a society divided into two very harmoniously complementary moieties, the Céra and the Tugaré. The Céra live in the northern half of the village; their heroes in Bororo mythology are the representatives of civilised nature, organisers, artisans and so on, while the *aroettowaraare* is a Céra witch, an intermediary between the living and the 'good' dead, who cures and is never possessed. The Tugaré live in the southern half of the village and their mythological heroes are demiurges, the offspring of natural beings such as animals or rivers, representatives of nature as wild. The *bari*, the Tugaré 'witch', serves as an intermediary between the living and the evil-doing dead, and is concerned with sickness and death. He is occasionally possessed by the dangerous souls of dead *bari*. Power used to belong to the Tugaré, who gave it up to the Céra, the representatives of civilised nature. Given this, a Céra can marry only a Tugaré woman and vice versa. But it is the mother who decides the group to which her children should belong, and it is the man who goes and lives with the woman. There is thus the appearance of ardent reciprocity and of a continuous flow of exchanges between two harmoniously overlapping but clearly distinguished moieties. However, the ethnographer observes, the moieties are divided into clans and the clans subdivided into three grades: higher, middle, lower. It is this hierarchy that makes social organisation real and which governs marriage exchanges, but it is not attested in the myth, which seems instead to deny or to mask its existence. The reality that the myth conceals is therefore that of three endogamous societies 'that, without knowing it, will remain forever distinct and isolated, each imprisoned in a proud isolation and hidden even in its own eyes by deceitful institutions'.[28] Catherine Backès-Clément observes that Lévi-Strauss's thought is not so far removed from that of Marx here, in holding that, although the forces of nature are not really dominated, mythology dominates them through the imagination.

The contradiction that the Bororo myth would tend to resolve or conceal is of an economic or social order. Catherine Backès-Clément has no difficulty in showing how, from *Structural Anthropology* onwards, Lévi-Strauss is increasingly interested in myth for its own sake, in as much as it represents a logical instrument well-suited to resolve contradictions. But these contradictions no longer refer necessarily to particular social and economic conditions. They are of an intellectual order and arise out of the opposition between nature and culture (raw and cooked, honey and ashes). Whether they touch on sensible qualities, on forms, or on relations, the logic of myths proceeds by oppositions, divisions and reversals that continue until all the possible formulae of composition and recomposition are exhausted. Myths would here be comparable with anthropology in general, in that (as Lévi-Strauss admitted in *Tristes Tropiques*) it studies a process of disintegration (an attitude that, as we have seen, would seem to inform all his attempts to define and clarify the notion of progress). 'Myths', writes Catherine Backès-Clément, 'lead by way of detours through more and more refined logical forms, with regard to both content and analysis, not to meaning but to the *absence of meaning.*' Thus myths, like music, would work through their emotive power (this assertion of non-meaning almost allows one to assert the priority of function and thus to occupy a position similar to that of Victor Turner, as we shall see below).

But this is clearly not the crucial point. What is crucial for Lévi-Strauss is to show that all the possibilities of philosophical and technical thought are already present in the 'savage' mind, but in some sense in an unconscious state. Only contingent happenings (the 'Greek miracle' would serve to show the irreducibly contingent character of events) guarantee the passage to consciousness (understood as the detachment of logical representations from the concrete experience in which they are rooted), which is also the passage to scientific thought. But the reader is still left a little uncertain as to the essence of Lévi-Strauss's argument: why is the concrete root of myth sometimes the actual social order, the one that is characteristic of such and such a society, and sometimes the original elements of nature and culture in general? Why is the category 'unconscious' applied indiscriminately both to the general laws of the human mind and to the possible systematisations that are outside the field of experience of the individuals or societies observed (the systematicity of elementary structures, the laws governing the transformation of a corpus of myths), to the functions of concealment and occultation by means of which myths apparently guarantee the maintenance of a given social order, and to the actual logic of the relations that are set up, dissolved and reconstituted by the myth? Is it that these things are unconscious of existing outside the external realities whose image they manipulate?

Without providing a direct answer to these questions I would like to advance several lines of thought regarding Lévi-Strauss's notion of the symbolic order, in the hope that these will help us to formulate some answers. In his 'Introduction à l'œuvre de Marcel Mauss', economics, as much as kinship and religion, is designated by Lévi-Strauss as symbolic.[29] This assertion seems to me a crucially important one, in as much as it suggests that all these systems, as symbolic systems, must be considered of equivalent standing. But this is precisely what Lévi-Strauss does not do in his books; everything in fact happens as if he considered that, on the one hand, certain aspects of social-symbolic life refer to practice, whilst others are expressive (thus we observe that he is more concerned with myths than with rites, but that he only mentions symbolic efficacy when he is concerned with shamanistic ritual),[30] and on the other hand certain levels of symbolic organisation are, in terms of causality, subordinated to others. We have seen that the Bororo myth in *Tristes Tropiques* really did seem like a 'superstructure', reflecting and deforming real social organisation. I would note here that this rigorously Marxist schema of structures, superimposed one on top of another, may well always be in the background of structuralist theory, which would explain why Lévi-Strauss himself sees no incompatibility in principle between his own analytic procedures and those of Marxism. Nor is there, from this point of view, any incompatibility between his analysis of the Bororo myth in *Tristes Tropiques* and the analyses in *Mythologies*; the fact that the latter do not refer to a socio-economic reality but reveal internal logical schemata does not make them *a priori* incompatible with the further project of relating a myth's content to another level of reality. Lévi-Strauss has asserted in a wider sense, the possibility of a project of this sort,[31] and here I differ both from Catherine Backès-Clément ('so it is that, from structure to structure, the real could clearly disappear as cause, and in the not too distant future Lévi-Strauss will reduce the real to being only one code among several, and myth will assume a dominant place in a generalised system of correspondences') and from Castoriadis. It seems to me quite reasonable to suppose that the fact that myths think themselves is in no sense incompatible, in Lévi-Strauss's terms, with the fact that one may think them in relation to something else.

My objection to his arguments would tend rather to stem from the fact that he does not draw all the conclusions that he might from his definition of symbolic systems and from the fact that he considers some to be in some way more (or less) symbolic than others. If economy, kinship, religion, etc., constitute so many symbolic systems of equal 'dignity', there can be no question either of studying their logic exclusively, or of taking some to reflect, with greater or lesser degrees of sophistication, the others. The articulation of symbolic systems can only be thought in relation to the practices that set them going, and which in fact appeal, even in the case of the most anodyne among them, to all the registers of social life. A logic of symbolic practices, if it is possible, ought at first to be tackled in relation to a particular society: it can only be defined at the outset as a function of relations actually linking social actors, as a function of their status and situation, in a concrete society. The customary distinctions between the observer's model and the practice of the observed, and between symbolic expression and function, would thereby again come to be undermined. One would in addition want to know if there was a logical structure common to the particular symbolic logics in their entirety.

But a project of this sort, that would clearly tend not to dissociate structure and symbolic efficacy, logic and history, works by putting different symbolic registers on the same *level*. It seems to me that Lévi-Strauss, because he has been influenced, more or less consciously, by the now classic schema of the *verticality* of social 'instances', endows the symbolic sets that he studies with a greater or lesser measure of signification and of functionality (alliance structures refer by definition to practices, ritual has an immediate finality, myth has more capacity to be a site for intellectual speculation and 'representation' of the world). In this respect structuralism is not so far removed from functionalism, and it too fails to establish a genuine theory of symbolic efficacy and a genuine relation between the notions of symbol and ideology.

The answer may yet again be that structuralism's finality does not lie in articulating some symbolic registers with others, but in elucidating the logic of each of them. However, it is the very legitimacy of this approach that we can question. For social (or symbolic) logic cuts across these different registers and their respective boundaries are, as a moment's thought or the simplest experience serves to show, very indistinct. One will perhaps miss something of the logic of kinship and alliance if one studies them just for themselves, and one cannot give an exhaustive account of mytho-logics if one simply reads myths. Needham's and Leach's remarks are clearly pertinent here, in that Needham questions the self-evident nature of the pre-defined intellectual objects that the anthropological tradition offers, whilst Leach, in order to establish new 'structural arrangements',[32] sets up a framework for considering the systematic relations between elements that derive from anthropological categories customarily treated as distinct.

A structural arrangement could, for instance, be the sort of systematic relation that exists in some societies between symbols that correspond to genetic influence, to psychological authority, to modes of incorporation into groups, and to marriage alliances. If these 'topological' sets (which are never simply reducible to the reconstitution by the observer of models that are really operative for those observed) have a virtue, it lies in the fact that they constitute an intellectual object that derives from experience and one that eludes anthropology's *a priori* categories. But I am afraid that it is the case with Leach, as with others, that one *a priori* is being driven out of the door whilst another is being admitted through the window. He thus establishes a correspondence between the alliance relation and the notion of 'mystical' influence, but the latter is then taken to be a 'cultural expression' of the former, so that a game of mirrors – the same one that structuralists and functionalists invariably succumb to, once they try to theorise relations or articulations – is bound to re-emerge. In this game of mirrors, moreover, social diversity will not really feature at all. This implies that, at least in their being employed and uttered, symbolic relations vary as a function of the identity and position of those who use them and of those to whom they are applied. There is no homogenous and harmonious body of representations which is then used by all and sundry, with that body of representations seeming to be the production, emanation or reflection of an undifferentiated society or culture. A logic of symbolic practices can, however, bring out how it is that the diverse situations of actual speakers and actors are already signified in the most general symbolic configurations.[33]

I will now consider how those who favour a functionalist approach tackle this same problem of social order and symbolic efficacy.

Symbol and function: Victor Turner

Victor Turner is first and foremost a disciple of Max Gluckman,[34] and in this guise he strives to contribute to the comparative analysis of processes. His analysis and definition of types of change depend upon extended observation of privileged and significant 'cases', but, as Jacques Lombard recalls in *L'Anthropologie britannique contemporaine*, this 'case' method tends more to complement the structuralist method than to be opposed to it ('it may be true that one risks obscuring rich and unique elements when one reduces a complex reality in a structural analysis, but it is also obvious that an analysis is only possible if one elicits a structure'). It ought also to be borne in mind that the equilibrium model of which Gluckman speaks is neither a structure in the structuralist sense (it is simply a methodological tool that allows one to have an instantaneous, provisional and approximate look at a momentary state of empirically observed social relations) nor is it strictly speaking a structure of practice of the sort that Bourdieu subsequently delineates. The fact is that, in spite of the considerable interest of studies inspired by the *extended case method*, Gluckman and his colleagues have not really elicited a general logic of power relations such that they could have formulated a more systematic theory of 'social control', a recurrent theme in Gluckman's work and one that ensures its continuing relevance.

After *Schism and Continuity in Tribal Africa*, Turner produced two extremely rich books devoted to the study of symbolism and ritual.[35] I will pay particular attention here to the themes of ritual and initiation such as they are tackled in *The Ritual Process, Structure and Anti-Structure*, my aim being to show how the functionalist method at its most developed is significantly different from researches of the 'geneticist' type. These latter, as exemplified by the work of a 'historian of religions' like Mircea Eliade, strive to highlight universal functional levels that are liable to explain the whys and wherefores both of the cohesion of societies and of their marginal forms.

For Mircea Eliade,[36] initiation is defined as a 'body of rites and oral teachings whose purpose is to produce a radical modification in the religious and social status of the person to be initiated', and it is equivalent to 'an ontological mutation in existential condition' characteristic of puberty rites, of admission rites into sects or brotherhoods, and of those rites through which the vocation of specialists like shamans is realised. All these rites have a number of themes in common, and these guarantee their efficacy, in as much as they evoke and re-enact the inaugural cosmogonic myth. Of these themes I will single out those pertaining to the neophyte's separation from his mother, to death and symbolic resurrection, and those (complementing the previous ones) that pertain to gestation, ingestion and symbolic cannibalism. These are all basically variations on a central theme; Australian puberty rites or the Mysteries of Eleusis are above all a repetion of the cosmogony: 'Initiation is a recapitulation of the sacred history of the World and of the tribe. On this occasion, the entire society immerses itself once more in the mythical Times of origin and emerges from them regenerated.' If, therefore, a history of religions is possible this is due to the recurrence of a certain number of themes, a recurrence which may be explained without having recourse to diffusionist hypotheses, but by invoking universal properties of the human mind, i.e., that one participates in the 'plenitude of sacred, primordial Time'. Mircea Eliade thus considers that a certain number of rites are above all expressive of the human mind.

Without setting aside the problem of the rite's efficacy, he does in fact link it to the satisfaction that an evocation of origins would produce, whilst at the same time making a second distinction, which also features in functionalism, between a society's official and marginal sectors. In Eliade's work this is phrased in terms of an opposition between masculine initiation, as repetition of the cosmogony directed at culture, and feminine initiation, as recognition of the fact of menstruation, which is therefore directed at nature and, beyond that, at magic and acts of reversal that to some extent work to counterbalance the established power of men.

A distinction of this sort is totally artificial, as a whole range of examples would serve to demonstrate. Women often play a significant role in rituals that are perfectly integrated with a society's official functioning, nor can rituals of reversal (which play on the relations between the sexes or on power relations) be understood if one treats them as marginal and accessory phenomena. In short, the problem of initiation refers to the general problem of social structure in the institutional and empirical sense of the term, and Turner is clearly the author who has tried to give the most systematic account of the double reality which seems to correspond to it: 'normal' social statuses and 'marginal' or paradoxical states through which one has to pass in order to attain normality. Turner was inspired by Van Gennep's analysis of rites of passage, where he distinguished between different phases (separation, marginality and reaggregation) of passage from one culturally defined state to another. In a more sophisticated formulation Van Gennep defined the notion of *liminality* as the extreme marginal state, the typical ritual state, and distinguished between preliminal, liminal and postliminal phases. This notion of liminality allows Turner to define and discriminate between notions of 'structure' and 'communitas'; for him liminality would correspond to the periods of transition between the 'normal' or 'structured' states of social life. All social life would in fact be ordered according to two main models, alternative or superimposed, one defining the structured, differentiated and hierarchised system of political, juridical and economic 'structures', the other corresponding to a relatively undifferentiated state proper to periods of liminality, and defining a community or even a communion of equals, all equally subordinated to the authority of the masters of ritual. 'Structure' and 'communitas' would both be present in every form of society and would correspond to what Nietzsche, in a formula that has found much favour in anthropology, would have called the Apollonian and Dionysian phases in social life. For Turner, however, if there is indeed in every society a dialogue between 'communitas' and 'structure', nature and culture, it is finally Apollo, or structure, that brings about the unity of contraries. This analysis raises at least two crucial questions: can the structure/communitas opposition be held to account for all ritual activity? Can this opposition itself be justified, and can its characteristic paradoxes and reversals really be defined and apprehended outside of a 'structural' context?

The first question brings us to a problem that has already been touched upon in my discussion of the work of various other authors, that of the unity of rituals. Turner, who is faithful here to an Anglo-Saxon research tradition, seeks to discover the element that is common to the apparently diverse types of situation: that of neophytes in the liminal phase of initiation rituals, that of the indigenous people in a country dominated by invaders, that of beggars in a society, that of millenarian movements, that of monastic orders, that of patrilineality in a matrilineal society, and that of matrilineality in a patrilineal society, etc. In this respect, Turner's project is as classical as it is ambitious, but it is as fragile as it is classical. It is just one of a whole series of enquiries that have sought basically to oppose a 'structural' to a 'marginal' sector and to reduce this opposition, in cheerfully finalist terms, through an approach which results in the marginal being presented as functioning to the advantage of the structural. Descent and complementary filiation (Meyer Fortes), incorporation and alliance (Leach), thus define lines along which substances, powers, influences and a range of rights would in every society be transmitted, with everything happening as if one might systematically discriminate between the representations that societies have of the established juridical aspects and the spontaneous and 'mystical' aspects of interhuman relations. Something of this same quality informs the numerous analyses that Mary Douglas devotes to 'pollution', to defilement and to the interstitial sectors of social life, sectors in which marginal influences such as witchcraft would tend to be at work.

But Turner's enquiries into the unity of ritual go further than this, and it is for this reason that his attempts are particularly important for the analysis of ideological efficacy and political practices. For him there are actually only two types of liminality and two types of ritual, which are, moreover, closely connected: *rites of status elevation* and *rites of status reversal*. The first ensure the progress of neophytes through a hierarchy of institutional positions (this is the case, for instance, with puberty rites), and the second are essentially cyclical or seasonal rites in which persons occupying inferior positions in the social hierarchy can be brought to exercise a ritual authority over their superiors, this 'reversal' sometimes being accompanied by very spectacular demonstrations and provocations.

There are at least two respects in which Turner supersedes the sort of thematic analysis so dear to the historian of religions. First, he tries to understand the mechanism of ritual efficacy. He thus suggests that the symbolism of rites and myths is apparently so complex and tortuous because ritual at any rate derives its identity from two sources, one of which is physiological, the other social and moral. The drives and emotions that stem from human physiology and are aroused by ritual forms would therefore guarantee the passage from the obligatory to the desirable that, in Durkheim's terms, was the essence of the religious function. In constituting the unity of the affective and the somatic with the structural and the psychological a rite provides its participants with a psychological aid, and in this sense religion is 'rational'.

Second, Turner tries to give an account of what ritual in general is, and does not consider initiation rites to be a subject to be analysed on its own. In thus transcending a simple empirical apprehension of an institution, he shows how the two types of liminality and the two types of ritual orientations (rise in, and reversal of, status) that he has distinguished, together apply as much to the definition of initiation rites as to that of rites of installation and coronation; liminality or 'communitas' are not specific to female initiation but are an aspect of ritual activity in general. Lastly, if cyclical and collective rites tied to production, the rhythm of the seasons, or natural calamities, are more often the occasion for status reversals than are other rituals, they do not enjoy a monopoly over them; thus the naming ritual for a Ndembu chief combines both rites of 'elevation' and rites of status reversal.

Turner's great virtue (in this respect he belongs to an established tradition in British anthropology)[37] lies in his suggesting what a properly political language and practice, and one that governed ritual categories, might be; one can doubtless go beyond his analysis and wonder whether every symbolic language is not necessarily political, and whether every school of anthropology, whatever types of reality function as a starting-point for its observations (religious, familial or economic), ought not to end up revealing power relations, the different modalities whereby they are set to work, and the mechanism of these modalities. Turner's proposals do nevertheless give rise to three different orders of difficulty. It is absolutely certain, first of all, that ritual is never divorced from non-ritual activity, since it does in fact set it functioning again, fashions its hierarchies and is therefore not opposed to it as 'communitas' to 'structure'. Second, ritual itself, even in its most collective aspects, for instance in initiation rites, is organised or 'structured' (in Turner's sense); this is true of ritual ceremonies and it is true also of the institutions that they set in place or reconstitute. Thus African age-classes are not a 'democratic' counterweight to the lineage hierarchy, and whilst not reinforcing it, certainly do not contradict it. Finally, the spectacular demonstrations associated with the celebration of certain rites (sexual or political reversal, symbolic death and birth, licence, excess) do not so much signify the undifferentiated identity of the community and the abolition of differences as the passage to that difference which constitutes the social. I would note in this respect that rites of status reversal intervene at strong moments in political life, when a chief is installed or dies, during periods of interregnum or when terrible scourges threaten society as a whole; power is only 'played with' and apparently mishandled at the moment in which its necessity is reasserted – to the effect that the passivity that Deleuze and Guattari make out to be a distinctive feature of the despot (or of 'barbarism') in *Anti-Oedipus* seems more like a feature of all power.

In spite of an excessively rigid dichotomy, Turner can still help us to rephrase a problem that all anthropologists have difficulties with, that of the analysis of symbolism (should one talk of its meaning and carry out an exegesis of each of its components or should one concern oneself with its functions?); this difficulty in some sense reproduces (and amplifies) the ambivalence of power, which is simultaneously symbolic and ideological. Symbolisms profess to be universal, at any rate within a particular society, but they install those differences which establish the social. There are therefore no societies that fail to constitute precise and complex theories regarding the notion of the person, the psyche, blood, sperm, heredity, birth and the order of the world, through which an order is constituted which, beneath the appearance of being natural, is always already cultural. It is doubtless a failing of functionalist analysis that it divides the social in order to understand functioning: symbolisms bearing on the human person, like cosmology and cosmogony, never teach individuals anything but to recognise their own place and to accept it. In this sense ideology is already in symbolism.

Instances and determination: Marxist anthropology

Anthropology that is Marxist in inspiration has grown in France since 1960 and has rapidly divided into a number of different tendencies that may each be summed up, strangely enough, by one name. Authors like Claude Meillassoux, Maurice Godelier, Emmanuel Terray and Pierre Philippe Rey have each produced bodies of work that are finally fairly distinct and may well correspond to projects more divergent than one would have thought possible. The same could be said of a number of their contemporaries and fellow travellers, but this diversity is really cause for celebration. For it is really a remarkably positive thing that out of the generation of researchers whose thoughts in the sixties were focused on the achievements and problems of so-called economic anthropology (researchers whose average age is now somewhere between forty and fifty) no leader has emerged, or at any rate no body of work so provocative or overwhelming that, as is the case with structuralism, other researchers, before displaying their own originality (or in order to do so), have first of all to cut their teeth on it. The sensitivity or modesty of everyone concerned, their relatively slight literary production (given the length of time and the wide-ranging nature of their theoretical ambitions) go some way towards explaining this state of affairs.

But two deeper causes have to be borne in mind. On the one hand, there is the permanent presence, thanks to Lévi-Strauss, of a fruitful structuralist thought (from *The Savage Mind* in 1962 to *Structural Anthropology*, II in 1973, by way of the imposing series of *Mythologies*) and, on the other, the renewal, thanks to Althusser, of Marxism. Herein lies the paradox (and also the shoe that pinches): the structuralist enemy is always there, and even makes allies, and Marxists therefore use him to excommunicate each other (some suspect that a language that is Marxist in appearance only is used to camouflage structuralism, while others denounce what they see as the too-limited nature of anti-structuralism, and yet others admit that both were right). From another angle, the renewal that people expected of anthropology (for westerners always take exoticism to offer promise of renewal) actually came from philosophy and from Althusser. But Althusserianism itself later came to have the patina that a piece of wood has when many claws have been sharpened on it. The mechanical nature of the language of instances was thus denounced, but the relations between domination and determination, as taken directly from *For Marx*, were refined. With the help of history and fashion, however, waves of 'desire' flooded the sociological banks, and a new disembarkation threatened. This was actually a new Holy Alliance (Nietzsche, Reich, Bataille, Deleuze) and one for which the Marxists were quite unprepared. Hasty defences were constructed against it, whilst preparations for a counter-attack were made. On the theoretical level the strategy in Marxist anthropology is defensive or, more unkindly, one could say that its tactics take the place of strategy.

But one would to some extent be wrong, for the most serious of these enquiries is composed, it seems to me, of a series of theoretical proposals based on exact case studies. Marxist economic anthropology is in this respect faithful to its origins and to its precursors, by which I mean not only Marx but also the more recent contributions from other disciplines that H. Moniot has very clearly summarised:[38] the anthropology of 'techniques' that in France has been hallowed by André Leroi-Gourhan's definitive work, the dynamic sociology of George Balandier (because of its break with an intellectualist and idealist tradition), the concepts contained in 'development' studies (such as one can occasionally find in monographs and as formulated in Samir Amin's work), American economic anthropology and, more particularly, Polanyi and the substantivist school, the rediscovery of, and commentary on, texts by Marx that refer to pre-capitalist societies, and

Althusser's rereading of Marx. These influences all indicate a twofold concern, with the concrete and with coherence. This concern may also be identified in a number of individual or collective works that no Marxist school could appropriate or claim in their entirety, but whose authors would acknowledge as arising out of considerations on Marxism. Thus Marxism has encouraged the growth of new methods and forms of knowledge concerning a number of anthropology's basic problems (relations of power and exploitation in lineage societies, the problem of the origin of the State and more particularly the relations between long-distance commerce and the constitution of the State, the significance of slavery in pre-colonial societies). More precisely, we can now completely rephrase the 'problem' of the relations between anthropology and history; in a country like France, where economic history does not exist as a specific discipline, it is significant that only the anthropologists who are thoroughly integrated within the Marxist current, or have in some way engaged with it, have decided not to discuss the relations between history and anthropology, but to practise history.[39]

This said, Marxist anthropology has a twofold claim on our interest here, for it may be both aligned with, and distinguished from, structuralist and functionalist problematics. First, it seeks to establish a system for interpreting the socio-economic functioning of the different types of social formation – a system which places in question the different 'instances' of socio-economic reality considered as solidary, and which provides a firm basis for the study of transition or change. Second, and this is a point that is closely linked to the first one, it seeks to establish a systematic method for the study of change which is not therefore divorced from the functional totality of a particular social formation. The originality of the Marxist approach in anthropology would therefore lie, in so far as all its works betray the same concern for coherence, in considering at the same time both synchronic totality and diachronic logic; and in so doing it would substitute analysis of the effects of domination for that of functional relations, and the notions of transition and disjunction for that of evolution. It would thus shatter the anthropological circle and free itself from the trap of contradictory intellectual necessities attributable to anthropological idealism.

But might not debates within Marxism reproduce a similar kind of circle? The sheer virulence of the dialogues between Marxist anthropologists would seem in fact to indicate this. I would not dream of dismissing any of the arguments advanced by these anthropologists but at the same time it is quite clear that these arguments may be said, as a first approximation, to belong to two absolutely irreconcilable tendencies. Suppose we take some of F. Pouillon's[40] analyses as pointers here. Marxists have, he argues, taken issue with each other over several questions, particularly the following: the thesis of the primacy of the forces of production, the theme of the appropriation

67

of the forces of production and, complementing this, the problem of the status of kinship relations in pre-industrial societies.

The first question refers to the definition of *mode of production* as articulation of forces of production and relations of production. The Marxists want to know which of these forces and relations (and none of them would be surprised at its being presented in the form of an alternative) would have priority in determining the mode of production and the conditions for its change. Here one can contrast the treatment of this question by Maurice Godelier (and to a certain extent Marshall Sahlins), who has advocated extended studies of technology in order to give a correct definition of the level of development of the forces of production, with that of Claude Meillassoux, who, followed in this by Emmanuel Terray and Pierre Philippe Rey, emphasises the general conditions of the labour process (hunting – temporary cooperation – sharing; agriculture – stable cooperation – building up of stocks). But I would straightaway remark that the consequences of these respective options have not been altogether predictable. Thus it is Godelier who, invoking the complexity of structural causality, will come to qualify (or at least to add mediations to) the notion of determination in the last instance by the economic, and it is Meillassoux who, having given a useful introduction to lineage hierarchies, will propose a mechanistic model by means of which social and political relations may be deduced from the characteristics of production.[41]

One can identify these same theoretical divisions when the appropriation of the forces of production is considered, but one can also identify the same uncertainties as to theoretical consistency and as to the logic of oppositions proposed. Godelier takes the meaning and basis of relations of production to rest on the means of production – an analysis that, more specifically, he applies to the tribal community of hunters.[42] Critics have objected that this implies that the tribal group is an indissoluble entity, that it has a political harmony and a basic egalitarianism (defined as 'general and reciprocal cooperation'), and that this rules out the possibility of locating, within a 'dominant social relation', the site of a contradiction which would be 'the actual mainspring of the system's reproduction, and through its development, of that system's disruption'.[43]

I would myself accept the first point without endorsing all the consequences that might be thought to flow from it. For it is one thing to stress the risks of considering a society to be an undifferentiated subject, and therefore to acknowledge that the analyses of Meillassoux, Terray and Rey have the virtue of eradicating the mythical image of primitive communism such as it may be found in Marx. But it is quite another to seek to identify, in a dominant social relation, the site of a contradiction that would be inscribed like some genetic destiny in the structure of a social formation, in this case the tribal community. I would simply point out here that a fair number of hunter-gatherers seem to have waited a long time for the development of a contradiction which is only emerging today with the massive irruption of global capitalism. This is an important point for discussion and one that curiously enough has not been at the forefront of debates between Marxists. One could doubtless contrast a 'Godelier line' with a 'Meillassoux line', in so far as the former seems to hold that the disruption of the system may stem, not from its intrinsic development, but either from an external event (contact, diffusion, colonisation) or from an event internal to the society but which is not necessarily the expression of a contradiction in it[44] (demographic change, ecological change that is natural or a consequence of human intervention).

Societies that are more obviously differentiated than hunting and gathering ones pose a similar problem. I am thinking of societies of the lineage type, whose fundamentally hierarchised character has been more forcefully demonstrated by authors like Pierre Philippe Rey than by Meillassoux or Terray. It is not argued (and perhaps an author like Terray would no longer say it) that forms of lineage society are in themselves bearers of contradictions that would be liable to culminate in the society's disruption. It is doubtless in this context that the term-for-term transposition of an analysis applied by preference to capitalist society (and that, in the last analysis, history alone can validate) testifies to a degree of Europocentrism.

But Meillassoux, and those that take their inspiration from him are still to my mind right in stressing the determinate importance of the appropriation of men in the internal articulation of the social structure. More specifically, Terray has laid stress on the relations of production that are set up in the context of collective labour, and Rey has emphasised the sort of relations between men that are established over the control of the circulation of women, of captives and dependants.[45] A second debate, bearing on the pertinence of the concept of class when applied to the elder/junior relation in lineage societies, has been grafted on to these analyses. If, for Rey, the dominant relation characteristic of the lineage mode of production is a class relation, it is because the latter corresponds to the exploitation of juniors by elders, i.e., the extortion of a surplus that is employed for the reproduction of the (social) structure of exploitation – an extortion which is not situated within the process of immediate production but within the process of social production. Terray himself reckons that the concept of class should, if it is to remain operative, be restricted to societies in which the labour/non-labour opposition is pertinent. One ought to add here that, for both of them, at least if their writing is anything to go by, the elder/junior opposition is still a relative one, since every junior will one day become an elder. It is also worth asking whether the organisation of lineage societies, which is inseparable in this respect from its conceptions of heredity, of the psyche and of inheritance, does not tend rather to create preferential lines for the transmission of 'elderhood' – or, if you wish, of lineage power; one ought certainly to distinguish between accession to adulthood (i.e., as judged in terms of age) and accession to elderhood, in so far as this latter term implies a social (lineage) power. Let me put it that, just as there are social juniors in lineage societies (to revive an expression of Meillassoux's that is applied to the various categories of dependant, and especially to slaves, whose increasing age does not necessarily entail increasing authority), so too are there social elders, who are sufficiently well placed in terms of descent and succession for their authority not to depend entirely on their age.

It is Rey who, in an answer to Pierre Bonté, has summed up the different priorities of the various Marxist researchers. François Pouillon quotes a string of very pertinent remarks in which Rey insists that the crucial question to ask is this: which appropriation is 'prior and determining in relation to the other', the real appropriation of the means of production or the appropriation of men? It seems reasonable to suggest that, since the modalities of the former correspond, in Godelier's terms, to a structural effect of domination of one 'instance' (in 'primitive' societies, kinship) that one cannot account for without reference to the latter, and since the modalities of the latter are linked, in Meillassoux's terms and in the terms of those who here align themselves with him, to the nature of the forces of production, it is not obvious that the relation of the one to the other is one of logical or chronological determination. One cannot help wondering if there is in fact a truly profound (and fruitful) opposition between two theoretical options or if it is a question of more or less involuntary misunderstandings.

An overall survey of Godelier's texts does in fact show that, although he avers the need to register the level of development of the forces of production as a preliminary to defining a mode of production, and not as the intellectual instrument of this definition, the possibility of analysing the internal articulation of the latter (characterised by the domination of an instance) is tied to that of analysing the modalities of the real appropriation of the means of production. Subsequently, and I will come back to this point, Maurice Godelier tries to define kinship in primitive societies as both infrastructure and superstructure, dominant and determining, but determined in its very being by the development of the forces of production. Meillassoux attempts to link the apprehension of the nature of the forces of production to that of the corresponding set of social relations; while Terray[46] tries to make this approach more systematic and asks that one enumerate the modes of production in a social formation, starting with forms of cooperation which should serve as indices for identifying them. But all these social relations are, in addition, considered here to be determined by the modalities of appropriation of men, which are also an aspect of them. It is, moreover, significant that on this point Godelier's criticisms are similar to the ones that Rey makes. Godelier[47] rebukes Terray for confusing the labour process with the production process and, in the last analysis, for discovering as many

70

modes of production as there are labour processes, in order to remain faithful to Althusser's definition of a social formation as the articulation of at least two modes of production; he thus levels the same accusation of 'technicism' at Terray as might previously have been levelled at him.

Rey's criticism of Terray[48] bears on the fact that Terray's analysis concerns the immediate process of production, while the dominant social relation can only be grasped in the process of reproduction: in the lineage mode of production it is the elders who control, along with the circulation of marriage goods, that of women and captives. One can therefore see why Rey, having understood all the consequences of Meillassoux's opposition between elders and juniors (an opposition that, as Meillassoux had clearly shown, did not turn on the monopoly of a material or coercive force that was controlled by the former and used against the latter), should emphasise the determining importance of circulation and reproduction, and should criticise those who had formulated this position in terms reminiscent of those they had themselves used to criticise Godelier.

One is left with the impression, in the end, of a four-cornered game (nature of the forces of production, level of development of those same forces, appropriation of the means of production, appropriation of men) in which each of the players, provisionally 'home', can quite justifiably denounce whoever has stayed out of the game. But the difficulty (and doubtless the virtue) common to all the players clearly stems from the fact that each has in turn occupied this position outside the game; it corresponds, as it happens, to the impossibility that they have all more or less experienced of analysing forces of production whilst abstracting relations of production. But once one tackles the domain of relations of production, one is necessarily tackling that of a social symbolic which, when compared with strictly economistic notions of determination, introduces an additional degree of freedom or arbitrariness.

If Maurice Godelier's work is so immensely valuable, it is because he is more aware of this complexity and diversification of social reality and I do not find it at all shocking that he owes some of this awareness to the structuralist approach. It would not be outrageous to argue that Meillassoux's analyses would be immeasurably improved if he had travelled further upstream, as it were, and given a more systematic account of the diversity of natural milieux and of technical conditions of production (a diversity which does, for example, make it impossible to employ a general category 'hunter-gatherer' without first specifying more precisely the intellectual object of one's research, and which does in certain cases explain the greater or lesser ease with which the 'passage to agriculture' is effected), and if he had travelled further downstream and stopped attributing any reference to the social significance of kinship data as stemming from the most harmful and blatant anthropological idealism.

71

Claude Meillassoux's analyses of kinship data seem to me to give rise to two sorts of problem. When he denies the general character of the incest prohibition and disregards the existence of kinship relations in hunting and gathering societies, he is simply flying in the face of the evidence. This refusal (and it really is a question of a refusal) seems to me to be remarkably significant. Once one claims to give the term 'deduce' its full meaning, when one thinks to deduce the nature of social relations from the characteristics of production, one makes it impossible for oneself to understand the thinkable and thought nature of these relations. One is not necessarily jettisoning materialist analysis just because one recalls the irreducible originality of the social fact (of the human fact), which is at once a natural and a logical necessity. This logical necessity is acknowledged in all forms of social organisation, but even when it functions to the advantage of those who are in control of them, it should not be thought of as a mere superstructural residue, a negligible factor that has to be accounted for only when one has identified the *true* determinants of the system and of its reproduction. It is in fact a part of the problem that was supposedly resolved by being set to one side, as if the thought of the system sometimes came to it from the outside (from the observer, whose determinants would be very interesting to identify), and sometimes from the system itself or its surroundings, in which case it would be like a superfluous ornament, a bauble, or an atmospheric phenomenon, a fall of dew (a mirrored trap for a dreaming observer), that the sun of economic determination would disperse in a moment.

The artificiality of the passage from nature to culture has been denounced by every reductive materialist in sight, and this with a great display of truisms, but what else can it be held to designate but the originality of the human social fact? Edgar Morin certainly sheds no light on the paradox inherent in this fact when he tells us of the 'self-organised' character of systems, any more than Meillassoux does when he presents as a link of causality (and, in his terms, of deduction) the link between hunting, immediate cooperation and discontinuous social relations, and limited control over the circulation of men and women, or that between agricultural production, a keeping of stock and enduring social relations, and control over stock and over circulation. No one would deny that these sorts of link exist, but they give rise to two types of question.

How would Meillassoux define hunting and agriculture without appealing to the modes of social organisation that he claims to deduce from them? I am not so much concerned here to denounce a tautology as to stress the need to understand the forces of production/social relations as a structured whole implying no logical or chronological priority. And secondly, what justification does Meillassoux have for describing hunter-gatherer social relations as if they were in some sense the soft form of what would (later) be the agricultural lineage society? It was clearly a simple enough matter for Maurice Godelier[49] to draw Meillassoux's attention to the fact that it was actually Australian hunting and gathering societies that had provided the anthropology of kinship[50] with a particularly sophisticated body of materials. François Pouillon, in the work quoted above, is right to observe that the critical factor 'would in the circumstances . . . be the possibility of witnessing the emergence in hunting societies of lineage relations as constraining as those to be found in agricultural societies, where they arise as a structure of control and authority over the circulation of men and women', but this is, once again, to suggest that the organised totality of the socially given should, prior to all reconstruction of a genesis, be taken into account. Australian hunter-gatherers do not first have the need to move about in small groups in order to be given later, and *in addition*, the exquisite pleasures of manipulating their marriage and alliance systems.

The same sorts of observations may be made about the incest problem. A number of authors have for some time now adopted a sceptical attitude towards the assertion that its prohibition is universal. Needham himself suggests that only mother-son incest is very generally prohibited and that the important factor is not so much incest as prohibition in general – an interesting enough idea that, for want of a theory of prohibition, cannot now be assessed. Meillassoux, in his most recent book, errs in formulating some hasty and flawed arguments on this subject. I would therefore repeat here that there is no contradiction between a materialist explanation of society, i.e., the fact of referring the whole of a given social structure to the material conditions of production, and the apprehension of what it is that is social in a society. Simply because one conceives the incest prohibition to be the act through which the intellectual and material possibility of the social is installed (the possibility of ordering is achieved by symbolising differences and that of setting things up is achieved by organising exchange), one is not therefore attributing excessive significance to kinship, nor is one reversing the order of determinants. All the examples advanced by this or that writer to demonstrate that the incest prohibition is not general, or that it does not enjoy the same extension everywhere, provide the proof, *a contrario*, of its fundamental importance; without laying too much stress on the scattered and limited nature of the majority of these examples (which are flimsy enough when contrasted with the imposing nature of the prohibition and of the theoretical ambition of those who question its inaugural character) I would simply point out that the most remarkable amongst them do in fact involve reigning dynasties. Everything therefore happens as if power, in claiming for itself what it forbids others, were contrasting the logical and thinkable character of the social (the differences which constitute the social order) with the necessary and unthinkable (because 'natural') character of power. In these terms infractions of the incest prohibition may only be understood in relation to it and its socially inaugural character.[51]

73

If I hold that Meillassoux fails to give the account that he had originally promised of the articulated set of social relations in the societies that he studies, it is both because he treats certain aspects of social life as secondary, and therefore neglects them (perhaps because of the vitality of the vertical model of infrastructure and superstructure), and because he is prone to favour apparently deductive analyses. It does not follow that all attempts to grasp the articulation of the whole of a social system are fully satisfactory. Thus Terray's original attempts in this direction founder on the ambiguity of the concept of mode of production. If this latter concept should sometimes be understood, as by Althusser, in a restricted sense (forces of production and relations of production) and sometimes in an extended sense (when it includes the 'superstructural' instances which are supposed to correspond at least to the economic infrastructure), it is clear that the notion of social formation as combining several modes of production causes problems as soon as one takes all the superstructural 'levels' into account. To suppose that the familial, juridical and religious organisations actually in evidence in a concrete social formation are there because of a selection, a dislocation or a complex effect of structural causality, is to admit that correspondences do ideally exist (within modes of production in the extended sense) and that the existing arrangement of these organisations is only the consequence of this.

Perhaps the 'construction' of modes of production is unduly favourable to induction, whilst the definition of the social formation as articulation of these modes favours an excessively intellectualist and mechanistic notion both of social functioning and of change.[52] Rey has done well to raise (albeit rapidly) the problem of belief and ideology in the Punu and Kunyi societies of the Congo. His 'daring' assimilation of 'mode of production' to 'mode of exploitation' is only possible because of the exemplary analysis he makes of a privileged case, that of disharmonic societies, where the reality of the leaders' power is clearly expressed in the residential setting (in as much as they are 'fathers' of their descendants and of their dependants, i.e., masters of these latter), and in the lineage setting, where they exercise other authority functions (as 'mother's brothers'). But Rey's transposition (and one that he takes for granted or claims to have observed) of this organisation to the ideological 'level' is nothing more than a pure and simple inversion: the powers that the father as father has not got in reality are attributed to him in the representations to which witchcraft beliefs give rise, whilst, conversely, the power of uncles as uncles (which is in fact considerable) is belittled. Once again we are presented with an analytic model that is highly functionalist, and one in which ideology (in this type of society at any rate) is only there to guarantee the passage of the rest of the social order, if necessary by means of psychological compensations, and by inverting the order of realities.

74

This conception of ideology as inversion (or dissimulation of real social relations) may also be located in Maurice Godelier's work, and is admittedly prevalent in the anthropological literature, making it easier, as it does, to give some account of a range of bewildering symbolic systems. One can thus contrast a world of the night (of cannibalistic, incestuous witches who have the gift of ubiquity and who travel through the air and meet in the bush) with the world of the day, where men do not eat human flesh, respect marriage prohibitions, are only in one place at a time, travel by walking and reside in the socialised space of the village. Only a very static conception of things will permit one to set up these pairs of oppositions (which, though not always false, are sometimes a little forced) and such an approach is particularly irritating when it comes to describing practices. My earlier remarks, which apply to aspects of structuralist, functionalist and Marxist analyses, are again pertinent here. Besides, the theme of inversion, corresponding as it does to a notion of specularity (even if the play of mirrors produces illusions), is not always the basis of local systems of explanation, which may easily attribute particular psychic powers to an individual who in fact holds a position of authority, and may give a formidable image to the powerful of this world and duplicate in the 'surreality', as it were, the lines of force of the social reality.

We are again faced with the need to integrate apparently phantasmal facts and symbolic practices with the domain of actual social practices, but without postulating a solution in which a continuity deprives the symbol of its efficacy and the social of its meaning. Godelier has tried, and is still trying, to extend this argument by presenting the whole of every society as a set of functions. He holds that it is an effect of structural causality[53] which explains not only why such and such an aspect of social life (an 'instance', in the Marxist sense of the term, which will thereby be undermined as a concept) plays a dominant (plurifunctional) role in a given society, but also that this 'aspect' (kinship or religion) is at the same time 'infrastructure and superstructure'.[54] More precisely, the dominant instance (which, in primitive societies, is kinship) only precedes and determines the others in so far as it has the economic as one of its functions. It is then argued that kinship in primitive societies functions as a relation of production,[55] and that this is why it regulates socio-religious activity and serves 'as an ideological schema for symbolic practice'. Whilst on this particular point Godelier seems to take things further than Althusser or Balibar (in assigning the place and function of relations of production to the dominant and secondarily determinant instance), for me the most meaningful aspect of his position lies in a definition of the indirect determination by the economic that is not so far removed from their own; Alain Marie[56] is likewise right to mention in this respect the notion of 'negative determination' by the economy, as formulated by Engels and applied by Lucien Sebag to precapitalist societies.[57]

But the fact remains that of the explicitly Marxist writers it is Godelier who has, through his deconstruction of the metaphorical machinery of vertical instances (from which he has not, however, as some of his expressions show, totally freed himself), gone furthest towards recognising the 'ideal' part in every 'real', to use those terms whose relation he is trying nowadays to systematise (although this dichotomous formulation is not itself without ambiguities). This, I would argue, is the direction that research ought to follow if it is to stand any chance of throwing light on the logic of social practices and on their transformations – a task whose feasibility turns on one's success in thinking, without discontinuity, relations of meaning and relations of force, symbols and ideology, domination and determination. It is worth noting, however, that Marxist anthropology (though irreducible to such closures) may itself be described in terms of the circle of irreconcilable necessities outlined above. It is quite apparent that it favours the first term of the evolution–culture axis, but that it reverts to the second when it is a question of understanding the reason for such and such a mode of domination in such and such a social configuration; to the extent that Marxist anthropologists' evolutionism is not doctrinaire, the diversification of modes of production (or, in a more Althusserian perspective, of types of social formation) obliges them to understand specifications without consequently abandoning the project of establishing the laws of change. Marxist anthropologists tend to confine themselves to analysing the first term of the function–symbol axis, until such a time as economism proves itself incapable of accounting for the societies being studied; they will then have to understand the place and describe the sway of organisational realities which appear to be neither purely arbitrary nor mechanically determined, neither wholly causes nor simply effects.

Having made this rapid survey of the different anthropological models it seems reasonable to point out that anthropology's own investigations do to some extent tally with those that researchers from other disciplines pursue in relation to it. First, anthropologists admit that a total interpretation is required, so much so that, although they lack the wherewithal to do it themselves, it alone makes their project meaningful; the man does not exist who could apprehend himself otherwise than in society, and philosophy's recourse to the human sciences and anthropology's attempts to provide an overall theoretical perspective may be considered as two aspects of the same development. At some vague point in the future, when this process is complete, one can just about imagine that it will be possible to define every social whole as a symbolic whole with determinations, limiting factors, and diversified effects. All rational anthropological researches raise questions, albeit in different languages, as to why symbols exist and as to the modalities of their efficacy, and, from this point of view, none of the summons addressed to them from the outside is truly admissible.

We thus see, as if through a kind of immanent justice, those philosophers who solicit or who exploit anthropology being caught unawares by the same difficulties as it has to face itself. This is clearly the case with Castoriadis, whose highly useful and certainly very productive notion of the social imaginary culminates in an absolute cultural relativism. He thus holds that a society's imaginary significations represent the very things that prevent us from apprehending them from the inside. The ethnographer who would seek to understand the universe of the Bororo and to explain it from the inside would no longer be an ethnographer but a Bororo; he has to explain the Bororo in the language of Parisians or Londoners, and if these languages are not equivalent codes it is precisely because the imaginary significations play a central role in their structuring. The ethnographer would thus be driven to a sort of 'spiritual cannibalism', westerners having in some sense no other choice but to reduce the history of others to their total vision of history. It is perhaps regrettable that Castoriadis, having stressed the need to substitute analyses of efficacy for analyses of function, and having raised the problem of why those who suffer because of an institution cling to it as much as those who profit from it, is content to evoke the culturally marked and specific character of concrete societies.

Deleuze and Guattari refurbish a classical evolutionist schema (savages, barbarians, civilised) in order to account for what seems to them to be specific to the abstractions of the capitalist State system; it is against these abstractions that they reconstruct a coherent and meaning-loaded system of codes of inscription in non-State societies, thus unfortunately marring an astute analysis of our psychosocial realities (indeed, of our culture), a crude and hasty glimpse of the evolutionary schemata that are supposed to have led up to them.

The various anthropological projects and the extraneous enquiries which comment on them, act as a stimulus to them or investigate them, do have one feature in common; this is a feature common to structuralism, functionalism and Marxism alike, and of course to Freudianism also. All these schools of thought actually take it for granted that there is something hidden in social organisation or in social structure, and that this something hidden is in fact their reason for existing or the principle by means of which they can be explained. Their common precept is therefore to mistrust what lies before one's eyes. It is perhaps time that we questioned this precept and thereby reassessed the status of the notion of the unconscious in anthropology.

3

From moral crisis to intellectual doubt

Ethnographers, like clerics, are the eternal and sometimes saddened witnesses to a history in which they often pretend to play no part. They could be considered the Pontius Pilates of the intellect who, as professionals, would prefer not to concern themselves with the conditions under which those they study are directly or indirectly colonised, dominated or exploited. And yet the history of this century (and a fair part of the previous one) is there to remind us, if we would but take off our blinkers, that the history of anthropology is to a large extent identified with that of colonialism, that the properly distraught witnesses to ethnocide and sometimes to genocide are indeed *witnesses* to it, and that behind every development project there is a modest, sometimes mediocre but always determined, 'applied' anthropologist. This situation has given rise to debates outside anthropology, but still more within it, debates that are often confused and represent a more or less rigorous interweaving of moral, political and intellectual perspectives. This confusion, which often assumes the form of an ill-defined 'bad conscience', contrasts with the intellectual confidence and theoretical ambition of those anthropologists who are concerned with the laws of functioning of the human mind or with those of historical development.

This unawareness is common enough in all the sciences but if unchecked would be the ruin of anthropology. Yet things have turned out quite otherwise, and the expression of scruples of conscience has come to be a typical feature of anthropological discourse, whilst, significantly enough, enquiries into the legitimacy of anthropological enquiry (or anyway of anthropological objects) has for some time past given way before questionings as to its intellectual validity. These factors demand both that we produce reasons for anthropology's endemic 'crises' and that we provide some account of the form these crises assume, and the formulations to which they give rise. I ought to stress once more that we now have a fair number of testimonies on these topics, the earliest and most virulent being American (I have Kathleen Gough and Gerald D. Berreman in mind here). There are now several good accounts in France and, thanks to Jean Copans, a report and an antho-

78

logy.[1] French debates have also given rise to monographs and collections of essays,[2] whose arguments I would not dream of trying to reproduce in full here. I will simply try to delineate the various currents involved in the conflicts internal to anthropology, and basic to it, and to situate them in relation to the others.

The crisis or, if you like, the heightened consciousness of anthropology in a country like France has been marked by two (fairly complementary) sorts of fact, one historical and the other institutional. Research in the field, which is the basis of anthropological research, is not done just anywhere or anyhow. A first appraisal of the situation shows that English (International African Institute) or French (Office de la Recherche Scientifique et Technique Outre-Mer) institutions have almost always been associated, to a greater or lesser degree, with colonial politics – the instruments, in a sense, of an 'enlightened colonialism'. Some French anthropologists have a past as colonial administrators and in the English colonies it was quite standard for anthropologists to act as advisers to the administration. It obviously does not follow from this that the men who performed these tasks were either the best of administrators or the worst of anthropologists. But this state of affairs makes the call for exteriority or participant observation seem a little ridiculous, even though they have long been presented as the key words in a new discourse on method. To be more exact, it renders exteriority fatal and participation relative.

Having said this, we ought not to lose sight of the exact nature of the scruple it inspired. If it is not simply a question of moral indignation at the, at any rate, objective (and sometimes subjective) solidarity between anthropologist and coloniser, and if, on the contrary, there is some doubt as to the validity and pertinence of knowledge obtained under these conditions, any commentaries will necessarily have to be hedged around with qualifications. I will first of all try to answer some very precise questions. What exactly is the intellectual object of anthropology? To what extent do situations of domination and colonisation prevent the anthropologist, himself a member of the dominant society, from apprehending it and constructing its logic? What, from this point of view, are the institutional handicaps?

The object of anthropology

This question may be rephrased if one looks for instance at the relations between disciplines (anthropology, history) or close sub-disciplines (ethnography, ethnology, sociology); so unsure are we of the answer that other writers would certainly contest the actual terms that I have just employed. It may seem strange that I am only now tackling a theme whose contours my investigations into the anthropological circle seemed to describe and that I was trying to relate to the deontological problems of anthropological practice. But in fact the moral and political problem of practice and the intellectual problem of object and of methods have always been closely linked, and it is not at all surprising that the moment we tackle the first problem we are, as a preliminary, faced with the need to confront the second one.

The vocabulary, here as elsewhere, is not an innocent one. In his *Histoire de l'anthropologie* (1966) Paul Mercier distinguished between ethnography, which is 'observation and description, fieldwork', ethnology, which tends to give rise to more extended conclusions and cannot rest entirely on first-hand knowledge, and anthropology, which tends to produce a synthetic knowledge of all human societies. He reverts at this point to Lévi-Strauss's distinction in *Structural Anthropology*. Thus ethnography, ethnology and anthropology would be distinguishable from the other human sciences, and from each other, not because of the particular attention they pay to a certain type of society, but because of their separate perspectives. The most complex and extreme questions arise with respect to the relations between ethnology and anthropology on the one hand, and sociology on the other. For some, as we know only too well (in spite of more or less strident disclaimers), this distinction refers to distinct empirical objects (primitive societies and developed societies); taken to its logical conclusion, ethnology would be the science of observers, observing the others, and sociology that of observers observing themselves. Lévi-Strauss rejects this distinction between empirical objects but to some extent reintroduces it with the notion of *authenticity*.

He rejects it in so far as he defines the difference between sociology and anthropology as being a difference in perspective: in the former one would systematically adopt the observer's point of view, whether one takes the observer's society or a society of the same type as object (be it urban, rural or religious), or whether one attempts more far-reaching syntheses:

> In his endeavour to elicit interpretations and significations, it is *his own society* that he is primarily concerned to explain: it is his own logical categories, his own historical perspectives that he applies to the ensemble. When a French sociologist of the twentieth century elaborates a general theory of life in society, it will always seem, and quite justifiably (for this distinction implies no criticism on my part), to be the work of a French sociologist of the twentieth century.

Lévi-Strauss's sociologist is here akin to Castoriadis's western ethnologist, in that his task is not to turn himself into a Bororo (presuming that he is capable of it) but to translate what he has perceived of Bororo reality into the languages of Parisians and Londoners.

If anthropology, as Lévi-Strauss understands it, does not succumb to this mutual incommunicability of languages and to this irreducibility of particular cultures, it is primarily because of its projects and its methods. The anthropologist lays claim to a particular type of *objectivity*: 'It is not merely a matter of rising above the values proper to the observer's society or group, but of its *methods of thought*; to arrive at a valid formulation, not just for an honest and objective observer, but for all possible observers. The anthropologist does not merely silence his own sentiments, but fashions new mental categories as well.' This ideal of objectivity is, however, not identical to the one entertained by the other social sciences, like economics or demography; the realities analysed by such sciences are in fact meaningless 'at the level of the subject's lived experience', whilst anthropology aims at the level of reality 'at which phenomena preserve a human significance and remain comprehensible, intellectually and sentimentally, to an individual consciousness'. These assertions, made in 1958, in *Structural Anthropology*, may well be incompatible with some of Lévi-Strauss's previous and subsequent usage of the category of the unconscious, but they do tend to define anthropology as a *semiological* science, sharing with linguistics the concern 'not to detach the objective bases of language, i.e., the aspect of *sound*, from its signifying function, the aspect of *meaning*'.

One can sense an echo of a debate initiated in another context, and bearing on the sort of 'meaning' referred to here. In support of his own definition, Lévi-Strauss quotes a remark that Jean-Paul Sartre had made in *Les Temps Modernes*[3] when criticising the fragmentary nature of sociology: 'The sociology of primitive societies is never vulnerable to these objections. For there one studies real signifying *ensembles*.' But it remains to be seen who deserves this praise, sociology or the primitives, the method or the object, or, if you like, the intellectual or the empirical object. Certain of Lévi-Strauss's remarks do indeed imply that signifying virtue belongs more particularly to some societies (or to some sectors of some societies) than to others. Lévi-Strauss is not happy merely to protest against the sorts of lack that are usually taken to define 'primitive' societies (*un*civilised, *without* writing), but goes on to emphasise the positive qualities to which these lacks correspond. This means that, when his demonstration is finished, it is so-called modern societies that could as well be defined by what they lack, and in particular, could be judged in terms of the criterion of *authenticity*. He observes that the societies that anthropologists prefer to study 'are based, far more than others, on personal relations and on concrete relations between individuals'; the limited size of these societies, Lévi-Strauss adds, allows such relations to exist and 'even in the case where societies of this type are too extensive or dispersed, the relations between those individuals who are furthest removed from each other are based on the most direct relations, for which kinship generally provides the model'. 'Levels of authenticity' do exist in modern societies (villages, businesses, neighbourhoods in large cities) but this authenticity disappears after a certain demographic threshold, when 'the social reality of "senders" and "receivers" (to use the language of communications theory) disappears behind the complexity of "codes" and "relays"'. The difference between anthropology and the other social sciences would therefore in the last analysis refer to 'two different modalities of social existence', with anthropology's object being constructed as a function of its (demographic) size and level of reality (communication), such that it would in the majority of cases correspond with the set of primitive societies.

Two things occur to me here. First, this does clearly imply a number of assumptions as to the nature of 'primitive' societies, and reflects considerable uncertainty about their delimitation. Second, it defines an ideal of totality and inclusiveness and a level of reality whose importance I wholly accept; if I do not entirely subscribe to these definitions (as I have partly explained above) I nonetheless feel bound to admit that a fair number of objections levelled at them quite miss their mark.

What does this notion of the authenticity of primitive societies really involve, given the glorious future that the artful friezes of structuralism predict for it? Why should the anthropologist not feel as much discomfort in the larger of the 'authentic' societies as he would in a town of thirty-five thousand inhabitants? It is surely because these societies are thought to enjoy a uniformity and legibility which those who are being observed, once they have the chance to speak, are quick to identify as being the creation of prejudice of the anthropologist. This at any rate is the kind of reaction one can expect from Africans with a philosophical training. Thus, writers like Stanislas Adotévi[4] or Paulin Hountondji[5] will protest against the notion of an anthropology whose very specificity is completely dependent on that of its object. The more the European anthropologist shows himself to be respectful of differences (and we should not forget here the current vogue that the cult of difference enjoys, whether in Jaulin's ethnology or in Deleuze's philosophy, in either of which cases it discerns the lost form of our own authenticity), the more, Hountondji informs us, he credits 'the generally implicit thesis that non-western societies enjoy a complete specificity, the unspoken postulate that there is a difference in *nature* (and not merely in *degree of evolution* as linked to certain possible forms of realisation), a qualitative difference (and not merely a quantitative one, or a difference in *scale*) between so-called primitive societies and "developed" ones'. Hountondji therefore holds that cultural anthropology and ethnology must owe their existence as separate disciplines, *vis-à-vis* sociology in particular, 'to this arbitrary division of the human collectivity between two types of society that they claim, with no proof at all, to be fundamentally different'.

A consistent structuralist would in fact object that anthropology tackles levels of reality and symbolic expression regardless of the type of society involved, but we have just seen how the definition of the criterion of authenticity is hedged around with ambiguities. I would also make the point here that the post-structuralists have given this same criterion unlimited currency by postulating a radical difference between societies characterised by 'meaning', 'code', 'territoriality' and exchange, on the one hand, and societies (such as our own) of abstraction, of 'axiomatics', of incommunicability and accumulation. It is clear what sorts of intellectual contradictions a system of thought will end up producing if it both postulates the irreducibility of differences and claims the right to give an overall account of them, as if some high-flying philosophers had alone discovered the transcultural point of view that would enable one to perceive, observe and analyse the reasons for, and modalities of, incommunicability.

But note the sorts of protest to which the apparently most generous aspects of the anthropology of primitive virtues give rise. It is quite true that the discovery of negro art and of the so-called philosophical systems of Africa had a progressive function in the first half of this century, for it revealed that those who were being colonised by the West and who were mainly used for waging war were not 'savages'. We should therefore take care not to arrange retrospective trials which would allow us a clean conscience at a cheap rate; nor should we demand of the ethnographers of the period that they have as fine a critical awareness of the meaning of their practice as some anthropologists, with the benefit of hindsight, possess today. On the other hand, those who are being 'observed' are quite entitled to uncover the profound spirit of imperialism which informs discourses that are generous in both appearance and intention. We should also note that these critiques are at once political and epistemological and that there is nothing moralistic about them. Hountondji's critique of the notion of African 'philosophy' seems to me to be the most radical and persuasive example of this.

All the implications and ambiguities of this notion are readily discernible in one key book – *La Philosophie bantoue* by Father Tempels,[6] a book that is still much read in Africa. It paved the way for a whole series of analyses that attempted, through materials like customs, traditions, proverbs and myths, to reconstruct a 'vision of the world' (a *Weltanschaung*) common to all Africans, 'subject to history and to change, and in addition, philosophical'. It is a simple matter to show how this rehabilitation of the black man and his culture is in fact addressed to Europeans (and to colonials and missionaries in particular): its last chapter is entitled 'Bantu philosophy and our civilising mission'. Father Tempels may be more talented than most writers of missionary literature, but he shares their ultimate aim, and the avowed purpose of his book is to prove that African philosophy was on the right path (the one that leads to a revelation of the one God) up to the moment when it strayed into the deviation of 'fetishism'. The basic task of a rational missionary was therefore to sort the wheat from the chaff, and to use his skills to reclaim and adapt the fertile aspects of traditional thought. Mission anthropology is thus the first attested and systematic form of applied anthropology; it paves the way for a mediocre literary form, and one that has hopefully not always had a real influence. This literature invents the myth of a society enjoying total unanimity and solidarity in order to set up recipes for modified forms of development. Hountondji is quite right to denounce the paradox by which one recognises a society's rare and hidden virtues only to treat it all the more as an object:

> Once again everything happens outside of the Africans themselves; 'Bantu philsosophy' serves merely as a pretext for a discussion between learned Europeans. The Black is therefore still quite the opposite of a spokesman: he is that *about which* one speaks, a face without a voice that one tries, with the help of one's colleagues, to decipher. He is an object to be defined and not a subject of a possible discourse.

At a deeper level, Hountondji reproaches what he terms *ethnophilosophy* for having knowingly confounded two senses of the word 'philosophy' as applied to Africa: the trivial, ideological sense (as when one speaks of an individual's or a group's philosophy, i.e., their spontaneous expression) and the technical sense, where philosophy is conceived of as a systematic production. Is Africa or, more broadly, are certain types of society, then supposed to enjoy the curious privilege of producing philosophy without knowing it, as Monsieur Jourdain did his prose? We should be on our guard against prejudices of this sort, for they feature in page after page of the anthropological literature, even when it is more or less progressive in inspiration, and they may well have some relation to the astonishing silences regarding the notion of ideology that we have observed in Marxist debates in anthropology.

No-one would think of referring to Burgundian or Picardian, or to French or German philosophy, except in the former case to designate in a quasi-metaphorical manner a cultural *habitus* presumed to be general, and to refer, in the latter case, to specific works, schools and theories within a technically defined field of thought. The illicit usage of this term in the ethno-philosophical literature stems at best from a kind of conceptual impotence, and from an intellectual colonialism as spontaneous as the 'philosophy' it claims to account for, and at worst from a will to recuperate and to exploit that one can still, even today (or, above all, today), find traces of, both in the theoretical elucubrations of the idlest specialists in applied anthropology and in the official political ideologies of *négritude* or of authenticity. The secret path leading to recuperation was opened up by ethnology. Tempels may well pass, thanks to what one might call the ethnological division of labour (a kind of scientific equivalent of the military division of the Third World by the great powers), for the great specialist of the Bantu culture area, and his reconstitution of African 'philosophy' may, after all, be the most obviously sensational of such attempts, given the term-for-term contrast it establishes between this African pseudo-philosophy and a no-less-imaginary European philosophy,[7] but there have been similar ventures on the part of other European authors in other regions of Africa.

Several examples of this spring to mind; in particular there is Marcel Griaule's book on the Dogon of the Republic of Mali, *Conversations with Ogotomeli*, a book now considered to be a classic of Dogon wisdom, and another, written in collaboration with Germaine Dieterlen, *Le Renard pâle*. Dominique Zahan[8] has let the world know about the religion, spirituality and what he calls the 'philosophy' of the Bambara, whilst Louis-Vincent Thomas[9] has carried out exhaustive research concerning the Diola of Senegal and has given lengthy expositions of their wisdom, their system of thought, or, as he too calls it, their 'philosophy'. Many Africans have followed suit, including various ecclesiastics (like the Abbé Kagame[10] from Rwanda, Monsignor Makaraziza[11] from Burundi, the Abbé Vincent Mulago[12] from the ex-Belgian Congo) who have been mainly concerned 'to find a psychological and cultural basis for planting the Christian message in the African mind, without betraying either the one or the other', and who, in order to do this, 'are bound to conceive of philosophy following the same model as religion, and therefore as being a permanent and stable system of beliefs, allowing of no evolution, always identical to itself, impermeable to time and to history'. A number of lay persons have also been involved, such as Senghor[13] ('whose chatter about *négritude* often rests on an analysis of what from 1939 onwards he calls the Black's "conception of the world" and what he subsequently, under the influence of Tempels, calls "the negro metaphysic" '), the Nigerian, Adesanya,[14] or, among many others, Kwame Nkrumah,[15] all of whom have the same thing on their minds: 'The passionate quest for an identity denied by the coloniser, but with the underlying idea that one of the elements of cultural identity is indeed "philosophy", the idea that all culture rests on a particular, permanent and unalterable metaphysical substratum.'

Hountondji's critique is particularly interesting because he is not mistaken in his choice of object. Aimé Césaire had already made a virulent critique of Tempels's *La Philosophie bantoue*, but this was phrased politically and in terms of a thinker's minimal responsibility to be objective: 'Since Bantu thought is ontological, the Bantus only want satisfaction of an ontological order . . . Hats off then, to Bantu vital force, and a nod and a wink at the immortal Bantu soul. And so you're quits. You have to admit it's a bargain.'[16] Hountondji is appreciative of the bitterness that underlies these observations, but notes that they do not resolve the theoretical problem; the actual existence of a Bantu 'philosophy' is not a problem for Césaire. Hountondji is in no sense unaware of the political dangers of an intellectual confusion that is liable to lead to an ideological one, but he is still concerned to distinguish between them, and in his writings, I would argue, the person of

85

the militant and that of the analyst are complementary but not confused.

At a time when Africa is torn by strife and when the gulf between oppressors and oppressed grows ever deeper, there exist discourses on the African tradition (and this goes for all those second-rate dissertations on traditional African democracy that are so rife in the African sub-literature) which are not merely wrong but actually harmful:

> If this discourse seems contemptible, it is not only because of its
> irrelevance and its display of indifference to the tragedy that is daily
> being played out in our countries and brings them ever nearer to
> Fascism, for every scientific discourse is, in a sense, equally irrelevant.
> It is also and above all because it has a positive function, working
> in this context like a powerful opiate, or as one of the key parts of
> the huge machine that is employed against our consciousness.

There may well have been a time when ethnophilosophy appeared to be a discourse that was useful for the liberation of oppressed peoples, but this discourse has today lost its 'critical charge', its 'truth': 'Yesterday it was the language of the oppressed, but from now on it will be the discourse of power.'

In any case, the fact remains that ethnophilosophy defines an intellectually non-existent object. Hountondji proposes the term 'practical ideology' to designate the set of practices, rituals and behaviours that seem to constitute both schemes of conduct and schemes of thought (not a 'philosophy'). He then makes a series of highly stimulating observations that demonstrate the close interconnection that exists between perspectives on anthropological practice and on anthropological theory. I will not discuss all of these suggestions here but would simply point out that the really subversive nature of his thought rests on his skill at discerning the real fault-lines in the social and ideological order:

> What first strikes one as being a group's practical ideology (in the
> singular) is never just its *dominant* practical ideology. Instead of
> hastily extending it to all the group's members, instead of naively
> taking it at face value, instead of forging a philosophical theory out
> of it that is presumed to have the support of the entire community,
> the prudent analyst will strive to uncover, behind the surface una-
> nimity, the whole gamut of non-dominant ideologies or, at any rate,
> relations at a tangent to the dominant ideology.

In thus relativising the irreducibility of intercultural differences, and in postulating the existence of intercultural differences and of relations of force and domination, all of which have been marked to a greater or lesser degree by an idiom presupposing unanimity, Hountondji is subscribing to an anti-culturalist project that does clearly go some way towards defining and justifying a form of intellectual optimism.

I would again point out here that it is of the utmost importance to emphasise the technical nature of Hountondji's remarks: it is one thing to emphasise the implications and presuppositions of a wrong definition of the concept of philosophy, but it is quite another to explain how it is that the object to which this wrongly defined concept refers is not what one claims it is. Hountondji does not dispute this object's empirical existence; he simply tries to specify what it is intellectually: a 'practical ideology' whose relative cohesion, homogenous appearance and underlying diversities (the dominant ideology *vis-à-vis* the other ideologies, or the different relations they bear to the dominant ideology) ought to be amenable to analysis. To emphasise the constitutive features of a 'practical ideology' (whose equivalent quite obviously exists in all types of society) is straightaway to highlight the lack of topicality that Hountondji acknowledges to be, in a sense, a property of all scientific discourse. One has to face the fact that with every denunciation of the sins of abstraction and theoreticism, one risks undermining the very possibility of an analysis of the social or reducing it to a more or less Manichaean, or more or less trivially sceptical, vision of society. It is quite clear that current opinion has no need of specialised discourses in order to acknowledge that people are wicked or that the strong exploit the weak. Yet criticism addressed to anthropology (even criticisms made by professional anthropologists) tend sometimes to suggest that it attributes to itself objects that are alien to the lived, concrete reality of those it claims to study. This position is, to say the least, ambiguous and needs to be clarified.

To illustrate this problem I will consider a particularly refreshing article by Claudine Vidal in *Le Mal de voir*, a collection of articles that arose out of two anthropological conferences held in 1974 and 1975. In this article, entitled 'Des peaux-rouges aux marginaux: l'univers fantastique de l'ethnologie', Claudine Vidal begins by introducing a number of wholly sensible observations, that are in striking contrast to the passionate declarations that she also makes. 'I refuse', she writes, 'to liken ethnographers to cops (even if some C.I.A. or Deuxième Bureau agents are ethnographers) or to treat them as compliant supporters of reactionary regimes (even if some of them are).' She goes on to point out, and to my mind rightly, that the mutual denunciations and accusations do not undermine the discipline ('they tend to make one believe in a recrudescence of activity instead') but that, in the last analysis, they are aimed at the wrong targets ('People talk as if their adversaries were free agents, and from their descriptions one would imagine them to be without institutional impediments, free to use ethnology for good or for ill, against imperialism or in its favour').

In the discussion following the article, Claudine Vidal makes three points, which are not all, in my opinion, equally perceptive. First, she denounces the tendency some ethnologists have to eulogise the past and to favour 'fully preserved' societies; second, she seems to want to compare this overall aim with that of theoretical anthropology in general; and, finally, she denounces the ineptitude and the lack of realism of ethnology. Suppose we consider these three points. A fair number of anthropologists involved in field-work do, by and large, conceive of the object of anthropology in terms of describing contact, and this is a conception that finds favour with those who consume popular ethnographic literature. When Hampaté Ba likens the death of every African elder to a library going up in flames, his famous aphorism refers to cultures with an oral tradition *and* to their ineluctable disappearance. The last of the Mohicans clearly does haunt the ethnographer's psyche and he is quite prepared, if need be, to fall back on France and to decorate it with a Breton hat or a Basque beret. Claudine Vidal points out that ethnographers have been in mourning for primitive societies since the century began, and that this perpetually deferred grief does, nevertheless, leave room for the ethnography of primitives. But there really is a contradiction here, for if Mauss, in 1905, was already announcing that primitive peoples were disappearing, what became of the pupils of the first (and last) ethnographers? 'They have continued quite happily', Claudine Vidal writes, 'and not just they, but the generation trained by them, and then the following generation, trained by the previous one . . . In short, they are still with us', and according to her, these same ethnographers, the descendants of the first ones, are still researching into primitive societies, with no concern at all for their life as it is now or for their history. This observation clearly does not apply the world over, and we ought therefore to try and find out just what it does cover.

In this respect, Claudine Vidal's analysis of Morgan does not seem particularly convincing. She acknowledges that Morgan did as much as he could to defend the rights of Indians and Indian culture and that, whilst he recognised that its disappearance was, given the all-pervasive business of ethnocide and genocide, inevitable, he did denounce and deplore those things. But she contrasts this Morgan, who was a skilled observer and a generous man, with the 'ethnologist', who 'fabricated' (to use her own term) *Systems of Consanguinity and Affinity of the Human Family*. This latter person seems to her to be in some way unrealistic, and to be preoccupied with reconstituting a vanished and phantastical notion of Indian identity:

> And what of Morgan's actual ethnology? It does not assert anything
> directly, with regard either to the present or to recent history. It
> considers those distant peoples, the Indians, and reconstructs their
> archaic social system. By dissociating former times from recent
> history, it creates an effect of unreality. The comparison between
> Indian organisations and the way of life of the Germanic tribes
> places them so far back in history and makes them seem so alien
> to white civilisation that these organisations, even if they were still

present and still implicated in present-day violence, came to appear marginal, strange, and dislocated with respect to the epoch. This elaboration of an original Indian entity, instead of exemplifying the existing one, tends rather to marginalise it and to make the original one seem out of step with modern times.

The general drift of Claudine Vidal's critique is clear enough; she holds that ethnology tends to particularise its object, to allow itself ideal conditions for analysis, quite regardless of any concrete factors, and to reconstitute lost states, which are really phantom ones. Researchers with such intentions do indisputably exist, but, in bringing these intentions to trial, Claudine Vidal is surely glossing over the most original aspects of the anthropological project. Here Engels, whom she quotes, would seem to me to have a better grasp of what is at stake in Morgan's analyses.

The aim of anthropology is not to describe societies but to study them, and the fact that description is the means employed does not signify that it is the end. What else can one study in a society, in the last analysis, except the particular modalities of the installation, functioning and expression of the social? Every study of a particular society presupposes a belief in the possibility of studying society *in general*, a belief in the scientificity, in certain respects, of the social *object*. One clearly cannot equate this belief with the assertion that all concrete anthropological research has necessarily to be scientific, but one can take it to mean that it is possible to locate and to order levels or domains of systematic analysis. When Morgan establishes certain laws for Indian systems of alliance and wonders if it might not be possible to trace them (or to find their equivalent) across the whole American continent or in ancient history (Greek, Roman, Germanic), he may be guilty of factual or analytic errors but his venture cannot in principle be faulted (since the very notion of a human *science*, at least as a thing to be aimed at, stems from it), except by those who reckon that social phenomena cannot be objects of knowledge. But intellectual nihilism of that order has nothing to do with denouncing the 'abstract' or 'unrealistic' nature of anthropological analysis, for this (like the relative lack of topicality mentioned by Hountondji) is a necessary attribute of all forms of knowledge.

One could clearly embark on a debate concerning the delimitation and definition of intellectual objects (I have, where necessary, referred to such debates, and particularly to those that have a bearing on the work of Lévi-Strauss, Leach and Needham, and on the various strands in French Marxist thought), but these objects can never be reduced to a simple recognition of a society's current problems and concrete conditions of existence. If this were so, a journalist or militant would handle the affair equally well. It is not that I question its importance, it is simply that such an approach is not comparable with the attempts at systematic knowledge within anthropology,

89

in as much as the latter does indeed offer access to systematic knowledge. I am only too well aware of the attempts anthropologists have made to study situations of conflict and domination and the realities of social change in their own right. But the real problem is, as far as I can see, to decide whether they have really succeeded in defining procedures and models liable to produce genuine forms of knowledge. Be this as it may, I would repeat: in spite of the illusions of earlier or present-day anthropologists, the object of anthropology is not to reconstruct vanished societies but to elicit social and historical logics. By which I mean genuine logics, that all may formulate, and not mysterious virtues that are as irreducibly unknowable as the cultures whose soul and essence they are.

Ethnocentrism and anti-ethnocentrism

I can follow Claudine Vidal when she denounces ethnology's tendency 'to fragment situations, to crystallise particular aspects of a social system, and to abstract them from their history'. I agree with this criticism, and would myself go on to denounce, along with the dangers that stem from hyper-culturalist illusions as she has described them, the taste for survivals and the intellectually ambiguous status that is attributed to them; but when she likens these more or less explicit attempts at constituting or (supposedly) reconstituting empirical objects (belonging to 'societies' or to 'groups') to attempts at constructing intellectual objects (like Morgan's *Systems of Consanguinity and Affinity*), I must admit to being baffled. I also fear that her denunciations of the unreality of certain analyses will be grist to the neo-evolutionist and neo-culturalist mill, and will thus favour the work of those currently fashionable ethnologists and philosophers who, even when they are exalting difference, are constructing an intellectual instrument for the most detestable of spiritual colonialisms.

An article, by Eder Sader, in the same collection, *Le Mal de voir*, 'A summary of anthropological studies on the Brazilian Indians', seems to me far more convincing here. The author denounces the spurious anti-ethnocentrism of the ethnologists:

> the thought that one should leave the Indian to his own logic
> conceals a vision of European superiority, and behind the respectful
> and egalitarian statement that "we have our logic, they have theirs",
> there is a reality – our extermination of the Indians. This real
> superiority betrays the hypocrisy of the relativist statement about
> equality. There is no equality, simply the superiority in logic of the
> one who knows how to exterminate the other. The recognition of
> specificity must not mask identities, and the scientific possibility of
> thinking them all.

I would add that this thinking of identities must not exclude the phenomena of domination and repression from its sphere of application, no matter where they are – one does not have to idealise the Indians in order to analyse the processes and the logic of ethnocide and genocide. Finally, I would add that moral and political stances ('ethnologists', Eder Sader writes, 'must . . . treat the Indians' struggles and resistances as if they were their own') seem to me to be more a consequence of the anthropologist's calling than a preliminary to it. Anthropology only has to be true to be subversive, but the converse does not automatically follow.

Those who disparage abstraction (for whom 'timelessness' is the supreme sin) and those who are infatuated with the idea of difference (for whom to understand is to reduce) therefore seem to me to be united in their condemnation of anthropology's intellectual endeavours. It is possible to object to this position on the grounds that, with the former, it stems from a bizarre intellectual confusion and, with the latter, from arbitrary presuppositions; but one can take this criticism still further and denounce a staggering revival of the sort of ethnocentric imperialism that is so common among French intellectuals. I have just suggested that Claudine Vidal's 'leftist' approach (she condemns ethnology because it holds that 'to be Commanche, Crow or Cheyenne is to be the incarnation of structures of kinship, marriage, exchange or of a symbolic system, etc.') rests in part on an incomplete understanding of the nature of anthropological research and that it also prepares the way (or, to be more accurate, it does not bar it) for savage denunciations of a supposed Europocentrism in anthropological research.

The only savage thing about these denunciations, let me emphasise, is their haste and their disregard for the consequences (where others analyse, they denounce). They stem from two theoretical tendencies that are actually quite closely linked, that of neo-culturalism, as elaborated by Robert Jaulin,[17] and that of neo-evolutionism (savages, barbarians, civilised), as orchestrated by Deleuze and illustrated by Pierre Clastres.[18] These tendencies have in common the fact of being vulnerable to the same sorts of accusation as they level at others. Ethnographic description and phantasy have never been mingled in so cavalier a manner as in the last three or four years, and never have philosophers treated such materials so casually. All and sundry, with great confidence and with a subtly arrogant condescension, scan other peoples' ethnographies (done by others, speaking of others) and decide upon meanings. If they speak of others for others there is never the slightest doubt in their minds as to what savages and primitives are, and the latter are thus finally rid of the inverted commas that used, owing to some scruple (whose motivation was perhaps just too confused), to surround them.

I would hate to be misinterpreted here. Every one of these philosophers and anthropologists has something to say, and I would not dream of reducing Baudrillard to his naive (or sophisticated) vision of the primitive world ('For primitive peoples, eating, drinking and living are first of all acts which are exchanged; if they cannot be exchanged, they do not occur'),[19] or Deleuze to his rigid evolutionism, which sometimes seems to be nothing more than a thing for his own amusement. Everyone would endorse Jaulin's denunciations of the mechanisms of ethnocide, but it is hard to take seriously the lyrical tone of a writer like Clastres when he defines the Indians as living in the future anterior ('Oh, admirable prescience of Savages', he writes, when celebrating the efforts of Amerindian societies to defend themselves against the rise of the State apparatus, even though he does not believe, or has ceased to believe, in the meaning of history). But his acknowledgement of the importance of politics in historical determinations (and, for instance, the link he establishes between the capitalist State and the practice of ethnocide, rather than doing as Jaulin does and linking that practice to the western or Judaeo-Christian spirit) opens up an interesting line of enquiry. The fact remains that all these authors are concerned to delineate the phantom of an ideal primitive society, full of meaning, still close to the most basic of desires and removed from the repressions that as yet only haunt it: the negative or lost world of a world (our own) that lives only for writing, axiomatics and capital. Thus the others gradually come to assume no other form in these authors' remarks than that of the shadow of our remorse and anxiety. They are a western product meant for the use of the West; their image is not fragmentary, as are those denounced by Claudine Vidal, but yet more unreal, and as undifferentiated and unanimous as the peoples whose representation in the missionary and anthropological literature so astonished and irritated Hountondji. Authenticity and difference are thus new myths for new ethnophilosophers.

Here again critical thought is contained within a vicious circle that it must shatter. Sometimes people contrast the elaboration of general laws with the specificity of different cultures, and thought is then equated with annexation. The nationals of countries that were formerly colonised rebuke anthropologists from ex-colonial countries for failing, out of a sort of masked imperialism or colonialism, to do the very thing that these anthropologists denounce as a strictly western sin, and therefore will not do. Africans like Adotévi and Hountondji are primarily asking us not to give a different meaning to the notions of philosophy, sociology and history when they are applied to their continent. Would we really only be able to choose between ethnocentrism and colonialism, between one ethnocentrism and another? It is obvious that the answer lies in a serious analysis of what one calls 'difference'.

Sometimes the elaboration of systematic laws is contrasted with the irreducibility of concrete situations, and thought is then equated with ignorance. Does this mean that there can be no study of actual concrete situations? But where would one then derive the past from, except from the speech of the survivors, that source of virtual coherence (I am referring neither to homogeneity nor to a lack of differentiation) that gives us something to think about? Does this mean that neither change nor domination are, strictly speaking, conceivable? But is this not to enclose oneself within definitional criteria concerning the manner in which the social is to be thought, that had at other points been denounced?

It seems to me that every radical (moral, political) critique of anthropology leads to an epistemological enquiry, or ought to do so. All the critiques surveyed above denounce, by different and sometimes conflicting paths, the whole range of particularisms (the study of situations reduced to their cultural or historical specificity, or worse still, reconstructed). They suggest that thought concerning the social has to be based on identity and totality, and Claudine Vidal would clearly add topicality as well. But topicality (which historians may try to find some means of recovering) is actually the totality of determinations and expressions in a social field at a given moment, and one can only think this totality if these determinations and expressions do not derive from a logic that is totally irreducible to that of the one who is doing the observing.

This is the very same question as I tackled above. Let me therefore stress that I would not myself reproach structuralism for its ideal of totality and systematicity, nor even, strictly speaking, for the irrelevance of the intellectual fields that it defines, i.e., those unconscious logics (which are in fact clarified by the institutional forms they assume) which prevent one from understanding kinship without alliance, or a myth without myths. These logics have their own importance – I would even go so far as to say that they are essential – and no relatively activist line of argument would persuade me that it is of no real importance to try and apprehend how men have thought their society, or to apprehend society as thought (which in no way implies that this thought represents or signifies equality or unanimity). Nor would any actively relativist line of argument persuade me that men think differently everywhere and that the underlying thought forms are absolutely irrecoverable. I would simply be inclined to wonder if it would not be possible to systematise the attempts that writers like Bastide and Balandier have made to assimilate topical facts to their conception of the object of anthropological theory.

Balandier, for instance, has used and developed the notion of 'colonial situation' in an interesting and original way. He has turned it into a wide-ranging model that, when applied to a particular reality, systematically integrates a whole series of different parameters. I would willingly allow that he has in fact constructed something akin to an anthropological object, and that his reference to Mauss (and to his notion of the 'total social fact') is, from this point of view, quite justified. I can also see why Balandier should have stressed that he was writing a 'modern sociology' of Africa, for his own work would thereby be distinguished from the 'unrealities', in Claudine Vidal's sense, that characterise certain kinds of ethnology. But for those who see no need to distinguish between ethnology and sociology (as opposed to those who hold, quite wrongly to my mind, that the societies studied by *ethnologists* are reducible to cultural features and to the innate virtues of the *tribes* that compose them), and who regard them as being simply the descriptive and analytic moments of all anthropology, the notion of colonial situation is necessarily of great anthropological interest.[20] The same sorts of remark would apply to Roger Bastide's[21] definition of applied anthropology. He would in fact take applied anthropology to be an anthropology of application, and one that would include within its field of vision, and in the construction of its intellectual field, the 'subjects' as much as the 'objects' of this application, the 'developers' as much as the 'developed'. In both cases, a new intellectual field is defined, and one that is not strictly speaking more realistic or more up-to-date than others, but is simply differently defined.

The lesson I would draw from all this is that the masked forms of ethnocentrism are not generally where those who profess anti-ethnocentrism disclose or denounce them. If change and struggle, domination and ideology, can and must be anthropological objects, this must necessarily depend on the anthropologist's capacity to give a fairly systematic account of them, and if I myself accord so much importance to the analysis of ideological languages and configurations, if I try to pose the problem of the relations between symbolism (which, to me, is not simply a matter for anthroposemiological interpretation) and ideology (which it would seem to me naive to interpret exclusively in terms of functionality), it is in order to try and discover the reasons for, and the mainsprings of, an efficacy that neither our epoch nor our society can claim to monopolise.

Scientific practice, militant practice

It is not that I would wish to denounce militant activism as such, it is simply that once one ties it to a professional practice, one risks falling into the same naiveties and hypocrisies as feature in the most basic applied anthropology ('Tell me whom you marry and I'll tell you how to develop'). Three different questions spring to mind here. The first concerns the status of 'objective' knowledge, and, secondarily, the distinction between militant and professional activities. The second concerns one's definition of a 'committed' or 'revolutionary' anthropology, whilst the third concerns the use those who hold power (or those seeking to overthrow them) can make of anthropological writing. These three questions are clearly very closely linked.

The most radical of the critical anthropologists are concerned to question the illusion of objectivity that is so much a feature of western anthropology.

94

The 'Friday group' have taken this argument furthest in their answer to, and commentary on, an article by Alfonso Villa Rojas.[22] The latter criticises the Peruvian, Varese, for assigning anthropologists the task of criticising false social and cultural but 'supposedly national' values that are imposed on everyone 'while in reality they are only instruments of power and domination'. Denouncing a specific situation, in which the particular interests of a minority constituted as a dominant group are opposed to those of the rest of the national society, 'composed of societies and cultures that do not share the same historical premises', Varese is prepared to conclude that 'the anthropologist's task cannot be limited to *ex cathedra* denunciations, but must also include the field of action'. In his criticism of this analysis Villa Rojas stresses the autonomy of scientific practice, which must be distinguished from forms of political action that each is free to choose as he wishes.

But the objectivity of science, the 'Friday group' points out, is relative; anthropological theory and practice have always reflected the interests of determinate social sectors. Science is, like everything else, 'a social product defined by determinate historico-social circumstances and, to this degree, relative and provisional'. As it stands, this radicalism would clearly fall victim to its own critique, but closer inspection will show that it is actually quite closely defined. It distinguishes between two methodological perspectives and two series of problems, the first defining a *context of discovery*, the second a *context of justification*.[23] The first 'context' corresponds to the 'framework of historical and social conditions in which knowledge, and the methodological and practical criteria that guide and direct it, emerges and assumes a definite form', the second to 'critical analysis' and to 'the rational reconstruction (at the epistemological level) of the products of all scientific activity, which must be submitted, whatever their field of application, to the minimum criteria of non-contradiction, correspondence with reality as empirically studied and the intersubjective testing of pertinent statements'. In the case of the first context, many anthropological studies are quite clearly based on a confusion between objectivity and an arbitrarily defined empirical object (a tribe or a village) and this confusion does affect their representation of others (a fragmented, sterilised, and I would argue, a hyperculturalist image). It is also indisputable that every science (there being no distinction here between 'human' and 'exact' sciences) is developed in an ideological context that is itself tied to a determinate historical situation.[24] Lowie did not have to wait for the emergence of a radical anthropology in order to demonstrate a correspondence between evolutionist ideology and the triumphalism of Victorian England. It is clear why those who live in the immediate sphere of influence of the United States, should be convinced about the mistrust that this relative conditioning ought to arouse in anthropologists. For direct attempts at exploiting 'scientific' information for repressive ends have come to light in the United States, and the Camelot Project, which was presented as a university enquiry, was funded by the State Department in order to measure or assess the degree of anti-communism in the Chilean army and among the people. Under these conditions it is obviously dangerous to have a complacent belief in some kind of scientific neutrality.

But here too we should take care not to replace conformism and error, however reprehensible, with mere confusions. Those associated with the Camelot Project did clearly show more naivety than taste for objective science, but having said this one still has to specify that the existence of a 'context of discovery' and of a 'context of justification' does not imply that in the former context science may be reduced to ideology. To imagine, as the 'Friday group' does, that scientificity or, if one prefers, rigour only depends on criteria derived from the second context, is to bring back a relativism whose disadvantages I have already emphasised. The history of the sciences is simultaneously a history of their errors and of their progress.

In the case of 'militant' or 'revolutionary' anthropology I shall distinguish between two separate aspects, the critical and the committed. That it is primarily for anthropologists to denounce a politics which, on the one hand, concerns those whom they study, and, on the other hand, is effected in the name of skewed notions of 'culture', 'development', of the 'nation' and of 'values', would seem clear enough to anyone who believes in the intellectual possibility of demonstrating the nature and function of biased representations. Anthropology's *critical* function seems to me to be an essential one, but also very dependent on its intellectual and theoretical capacities. The question of anthropology's positive commitment raises problems, primarily for those who advocate it whilst denouncing the relativism, ethnocentrism, racism, etc. of the anthropology practised by others. Does the 'Friday group', for instance, offer us any means of establishing the non-relativism of *avant garde* anthropology? We are instructed to cultivate our awareness of the world view in which we are steeped, in order that this consciousness 'should force us endlessly to adjust our theoretical hypotheses where it is a question of problems affecting men and of the attitude assumed by men regarding these problems'. This remark is really very vague, and their whole project very fuzzy, when compared with the vigorous criticisms they address to 'classical' anthropologists. It is not merely a right, it is also an intellectual duty[25] for American anthropologists to protest against the kind of 'nativist' politics that seeks to change mentalities in order to advance a 'development' whose nature they would not themselves be permitted to question. The 'Friday group' are quite entitled to denounce the intellectual laziness or moral cowardice of those of their colleagues who compromise with 'nativist' practices, but to liken these practices to those of 'classical' anthropology or to reduce the latter to being simply an accumulation of facts, anecdotes and 'exotic' behaviours, as some of their remarks suggest, is a far graver accusation, and one that, beyond its demagogic tone, is liable to culminate in intellectual nihilism.

Yet some who savagely denounce anthropology as a science would not hestitate to have each guerrilla flanked by an ethnologist, and it would not be a cheap irony to suggest that intellectual confusions of this order lead to an unrealistic politics. These confusions stem from the fact that some are clearly not content with the sorts of information that anthropologists are capable of providing, and they thus carry out the same reduction as research units or governmental projects effect. Let me repeat: if anthropology does exist, the anthropologist's calling is not that of an agent who gathers information, and if there are some who, after the sad adventures of proletarian science, wish to make us carry the torch for revolutionary or Third-World science, they testify more to the uncertainties of our epoch and of the 'profession' than to their fitness to master them. Some of Robert Buijtenhuijs's[26] remarks in the dossier compiled by Jean Copans seem to me to be particularly pertinent here:

> We should not have too many illusions, nor should we reverse the motto of the American secret services in Thailand: 'Ten anthropologists for every guerrilla'. I just do not believe that each Angolan or Vietnamese combatant needs the support of ten anthropologists. A. G. Frank is being more realistic when he evokes the image of a revolutionary anthropologist with 10,000 guerrillas. The American or Portuguese imperialists may need an enormous quantity of sociological or anthropological studies, but this is because they know nothing about the local populations; but real guerrillas do not feel this need so strongly, for they pass through the local population as a fish through water. Amilcar Cabral's publications show that the revolutionaries of Guinea-Bissau did their anthropological analyses on their own.

Whilst distinguishing between militant and professional activities, Buijtenhuijs nevertheless suggests that revolutionary movements represent a privileged object of research for anthropology.

This is akin to one of Kathleen Gough's proposals,[27] where she argues that

> we need to know . . . if the left or nationalist revolutions which have occurred or been attempted these last few years in Cuba, Algeria, Malaysia, the Philippines, Indonesia, Kenya or in Zanzibar present an *ensemble* of identical characteristics . . . I would be accused of asking for another 'Camelot Project' but such is not my intention. What I want is for us to do these studies, in *our own* way, as if we were studying a *cargo cult* or the *Kula ring*, without the implicit

prejudices that a corrupt financing of research implies, and without the postulate that it is counter-revolution and not revolution that is the best answer.

The reader will note that Kathleen Gough's objectives are consistent, at the technical level, with a definition of a genuinely objective anthropology of the sort that I tried to give above, but once again it is the definition of the object (and, following that, a whole debate on epistemology) that constitutes both the stumbling block and the culmination for discussions between anthropologists. A parallel problem, and one often raised, but always a little hesitantly, concerns the use to which the facts provided by anthropological research can be put. This is not a false problem, for we know of these facts serving political or repressive ends; but once again one has to add the proviso that it is not anthropology as such that provides information that can be put to use. Many other sources can be used like this. As for anthropological theory, even if it does succeed in providing a systematic analysis of the modalities of domination, repression and resistance, I still doubt very much that this would occur through concepts or in a form that was of direct use to the powers that be or to resistance movements. Anthropological theorisation is not a guide to action, a theory of revolutionary or of counter-revolutionary practice. It may give an account of these practices as objects of analysis, but they cannot be held to provide an exhaustive definition of its field of enquiry. For the rest, it is quite clear that everything can, to a greater or lesser degree, serve the cause of repression, and everything can be used to wage war. French geographers[28] have recently found that this applies to their discipline too, and in their work one can discern that faintly flirtatious tone and that grain of bad conscience that confers real intellectual dignity on a human science in France.

One can in the end see how real this moral and intellectual debate is, for anthropologists were driven to it by the cruelties, hypocrisies and intellectual flag-wavings of a period in which the business of domination and repression has, with the end of explicit processes of colonisation, actually intensified. It is not at all surprising that, in this context more than in others, anthropology should have political implications and that it should actually give rise (in bastardised forms that may unfortunately represent the essence of its institutional expression) to various practical 'applications'. Close inspection shows that the ethnological or sociological sections of the experts' reports in development institutes or other research units are often only there for form's sake. But it is also clear that the human sciences are attracting a larger and larger audience among administrators and in those milieux where decisions about political action are taken. This is particularly true in France, and brings new responsibilities for researchers, and for anthropologists especially. It is up to them not to set about reconstituting abandoned and savage territories within the frontiers of France, or recreating new 'marginals' and new Indians (youth, prostitutes, immigrant slum-dwellers, well-preserved peasants) who would be studied only in terms of an artificial insularity.[29] Claudine Vidal's fears are thus not unfounded, and anthropology could well grow several decades older whilst searching out 'new' fields for itself.

There is nothing fatal about this ageing process, as the example of American anthropology indicates. In an article reprinted in the collection of essays entitled *Anthropologie et impérialisme*,[30] Sidney Mintz emphasises the difference between the American and French situations. The crucial difference, he notes, lies in the fact that France had created colonies that were 'over the sea', and therefore external, whereas the United States had created 'internal' colonies, on their own territory. The presence of the Indians and the Blacks in North America gave rise to problems for which the European colonial powers had no equivalent. A whole range of other differences is linked to this one, that is, the fact that the colonisation of the New World had begun so long ago (when compared with that of Asia and Africa), the fact that American political preoccupations were purely internal up to 1890, the fact that a perceptibly different interpretation of the term 'racism' was given on the two continents. American anthropologists had in the end, Sidney Mintz notes, to reassess their romanticism about the noble Indian, and the crises of 1929 to 1939 did much to overcome their lack of interest in those colonised peoples who were living on their own territories. Works by people like Margaret Mead, Darcy McNickle, MacGregor, Goldschmidt, Herskovitz or Oscar Lewis seem to suggest that what makes an American anthropologist 'no longer depends entirely on the nature of those with whom he has to deal'. This argument clearly refers to the concrete situation in which ethnographers do field-work, but its theoretical importance lies in the fact that, in its call for a wide range of different 'fields' and in its denunciation of the distinction between the 'noble savages' and 'we others', it implies first that there is a form of anthropological analysis (and therefore of intellectual object) that is independent of the nature of empirical objects (types of society), and second, and as a complement to this, that every retreat into exoticism signifies both moral complaisance and intellectual profligacy. Sidney Mintz maintains that French ethnologists have not yet begun to try and apprehend a reality 'transcending the exotic', whereas the American situation seems to him to be much more advanced: 'We other North Americans are all half-castes and it may well be that in the end we shall have a moral advantage in world history, for our colonial past is so much a part of us that we shall never evade it by political legerdemain or by an escape into exoticism.'

The moral and deontological debate on the notion of anthropology is clearly reminiscent of the epistemological circle that I alluded to above. There is a kind of relation between the need to have a general theory of

99

meaning, which is one of anthropology's polarities, and the denunciation that some make of its abstract character. Likewise, the notion of function is nearer to being a preoccupation of those who seek to avoid abstracting the anthropological object from the most pressing and most concrete matters. The opposition between general evolution and cultural specificity also finds a concrete expression in the practical preoccupations of modern anthropologists. This overlapping should clearly warn us against confusing the different perspectives, but also against ruling out the possibility that anthropologists are themselves unable to abstract themselves from the ensuing debates.

The various enquiries that anthropologists have made concerning the nature of anthropology culminate, therefore, in a single question. This question concerns history, as anthropologists themselves live it and as it confronts them in a world that is both disordered and shrinking, both better known and more misinterpreted, both more uniform and more divided up into a multiplicity of irreducible relations of force, swept from time to time by waves of protest, in the name of meaning and of law, and by disputes that cannot be contained within the analytic apparatus of academic disciplines, owing to their novelty or to the novelty of their claims (on behalf of sexual or political minorities, immigrants, youth and women). Does history, because nowadays it offers new things for us to see, entail an eradication, an elaboration or a revolution in anthropology?

Conclusions

New sites, new stakes

For a commentary on present-day anthropology three questions seem to me to be vital, and the answers one gives to them are clearly very closely interconnected. The first touches on the specificity of the modern world, on its problems, on its modes of expression and on the characteristic appeals that it will sometimes address to history or to anthropology. The second refers to the nature of the 'symbolic' or, more precisely, to the new itineraries (whether parallel or convergent) that various disciplines stake out when approaching objects that are thereby redefined. Research in the field of epistemology is dominated, in the human sciences, by the themes of symbolic practice and ideology, but identical labels may well conceal (or rather, bring to our attention) the conflicting realities of an intellectual battlefield. My third question treats the theme of interdisciplinarity, a term which has long stood for the overall significance and complete interdependence of our uncertainties and our hopes.

I will now give a brief summary of my position on this subject, before discussing each question in greater detail below. I would argue that a number of realities specific to the modern world (large groupings, the media, business, new religious sects, regional movements, etc.) offer some empirical 'purchase' for theoretical research. This is not because these sites and movements define fully rounded objects of research but because they are themselves defined by relations of force and meaning that render them significant in two respects. First, one can apprehend the logic, the internal links, and the transformation of these relations, in various contexts. Second, and this is something more direct but not intrinsically different, one can understand the complex logic of the world about us. It is up to anthropologists, through their theoretical endeavours, to show us what their 'exotic' and their immediate objects have in common. I would also argue that historians and anthropologists do, to a large extent, have the same theoretical object, and that definition of the extent of this overlapping may even be considered one of the most urgent objectives of the two disciplines. Only time will tell whether the theoretical sector thus constituted (through refusing a radical opposition either in terms of space or in terms of time) adequately defines the domain of the symbolic, and to what degree and in what manner the sciences of the social and of history must, if this domain and its specific efficacy is to be wholly grasped, be articulated with those of signs and of the psyche.

Here, today

If anthropology has a place in the modern world, it is not because minority groupings are becoming ever more vociferous in their demands, or because there is a general yearning for some sort of return to the source. The spectacular invasion of the anonymous forces of capital has given rise to a widespread feeling of dread, and the current taste for ecology and for recent history, for authentic produce, literary works and landscapes, may be located as much in the variously cogent or instinctive reactions of the so-called 'average' individual as in the more or less developed programmes of parties, groups, resistance and protest movements. In being identified with a kind of history of the immediate past, the one that has just slipped through our fingers – leaving us with a vague flavour and a bitter taste of illusion – ethnology is enjoying renewed prestige. For ethnology seems thereby to delay the passing of time, and, more important still, to hold back time's effacement of things. It allows us to see yesterday's functional objects and to recover their beauty, to give speech to elders, to recover the meaning of lost configurations, and to give back a society its memory. This is particularly true of those societies and cultural identities that State machineries, depending on the place and the regime, are intent upon destroying – although the speed and efficiency of such operations will obviously vary. Museum work, the recording of life histories and hyperculturalist approaches can be seen as protests against the disappearance of a way of life, and yet this is not unambiguous, for they do themselves hasten this process. It is in fact the ethnologist's misery that he only appears in the cultures that he seeks to preserve, alongside those who bring about, symbolise or consecrate their disappearance.

The seemingly royal road that is given the sadly post-colonial title of 'falling back on France', is nothing but a dead end, for it transposes on to a temporal axis all the errors that anthropologists have committed in analysing other social spaces. If anthropological research is to have any urgency, it must lie in denouncing all those pseudoculturalist attempts at recuperation, which, in the name of a bastardised and idealist definition of culture, would employ specialists simply to gather vestiges of the work of artisans and of folkloric customs. It is not that I despise the ethnographic work or the attempts at recension and collection of documents to which historians and ethnologists in France are devoting themselves. A museum like the Museum for Popular Arts and Traditions represents a really remarkable achievement in this field, and one that provides both amateurs and specialists with food for thought. But for the historian, as for the ethnologist, archive work is neither an end in itself nor a funeral rite. To sift through archives, documents or censuses is to give oneself the means to think about the reality of the past and the meaning of a tradition. But the fact remains that Corsican culture, nowadays, is no more reducible to its tradition of polyphonic singing than is Breton culture to that of the weaving of flax. Moreover, culture in the narrow sense of the term (such as one reconstructs by means of a few objects and artistic, literary or folkloristic traditions) has never been the total (and therefore true) reality of any society whatsoever. If one reduces a society to its 'culture' one is presupposing that it is unanimous, as if artisanal, vocal or plastic expression occurred in a uniform manner, and one is imagining it to be solidary, communal and egalitarian. In the last analysis one is dreaming it, and dreaming it as if it were an antidote to the loneliness, inequality and coldness of daily life as we know it now.

Anthropologists are not purveyors of dreams, and they are not there to answer to the demand (or to the lack) in those who protest against the present, by offering them a kind of drug, a travesty of the past or of an elsewhere. Such exchanges are common enough nowadays, not so much in separatist movements (where culturalist illusions do, however, sometimes make headway, but whose claims nevertheless have a precise economic and political content), as in ventures that are more or less consciously bent on recuperation, and fan and feed the culturalist flame in order to forestall other conflagrations. Canalised forms of culturalist protest tend always to idealise the past, to condemn the State, and to formulate extremely vague political arguments. Such is the breviary of a moderate culturalism.

I cannot resist backing up my case by quoting some extracts from an article by Marc Aurèle Pietrasanta that appeared in *Kyrn*, 'the magazine of Corsica', in August–September 1977 (No. 78), and was called 'Actuelles'. It goes without saying that I am not concerned with this article for its own sake, but with the state of mind it so perfectly represents. I refer here to the invasion, by a gimcrack intellectualism good only for combining notions of primitive community with that of the Goulag-State, of sites where there is a concrete but complex reality (that of 'separatisms' and 'regionalisms') that is still to be analysed, but clearly cannot be reduced to a nostalgia for a lost way of life. Suppose we read *Kyrn*:

> Corsican identity only has meaning in so far as it refers to that
> original communal civilisation of a people who, in the course of time,
> have known how to develop concrete and direct forms of organisation
> and of collective solidarity. Therein lies the proof that our people
> knew how to struggle, with a great deal of success, against those
> who sought to alienate them, through the intermediary of the political

power of the State and the economic power of property and profit, as bound one to the other. Economic and political power have never managed to assume such a perfect form as on the mainland, and whilst property was recognised it had, nevertheless, to take second place after the widespread notion of collective property which never, let me emphasise, belonged to the State or to any collectivity whatsoever, but was simply the commoners' estate.

Even the most superficial knowledge of Corsica would show that its communal character is as relative as anywhere else. Yet the critical feature of the above passage is its suggestion that economic power, political power and property only appeared as accidents in the course of Corsican history and in a more subdued form than 'on the mainland'. In this egalitarian and prophetic fight against the State and against ideology, the Corsicans are joining forces with the Indians of the two Americas, such as they are dreamed of in hyperstructuralist anthropology; and this intellectual confusion (or complicity) has in fact gone so far that representatives of the North American Indians have recently met up with some European regionalists. If their struggles seem to them to be one and the same (as these encounters would seem to suggest), they may well think of themselves as having been similar (egalitarian, authentic, free), before the advent of the very thing that would retrospectively construct their identity, i.e., State repression. Marc Aurèle Pietrasanta thinks no better of the State than do the Tupinamba (as described by Pierre Clastres), or Deleuze and Guattari:

One only has to recall that nationalism, born at the time of the French revolution,[1] is an ideology that consists of converting the power of the people into the power of the State over the people (use by the bourgeoisie of the theory of the social contract). This same ideology has confounded Nation and State. Which is why the term Nation today refers at once to an economic market and to a political State, which are both of them instruments for the exploitation and oppression of the people.

But the forcefulness of the phrasing here merely prepares the way for a slight shift of emphasis and for a more moderate argument:

Would it not be better, in order to remove all ambiguity from the Corsicans' struggle, and in order that their identity should be protected and should blossom, to avoid this term 'nation', which is itself something of an alien imposition, and to use 'Corsican community' in its stead, which designates a far more authentic reality? . . . The Nation-States have paved the way for an intensified repression by a large number and wide range of different kinds of Goulag. Just think. That Corsican youth, just when it seems to be finding its feet, should conceive of a borrowed nationalist, and supposedly Corsican, identity as the fulfilment of its dreams.

This verbal juggling really does seem in the end to be based on losing on the roundabouts what one has gained on the swings; but what primarily interests me here is the use of images, stereotypes and allusions, which can as easily inform a reactionary as a leftist discourse, or quite simply a conservative one. The ingredients never vary: on the one hand, community, identity, authenticity, and on the other, repression, economic markets, and the State and the Goulag. Anthropologists may be held responsible for this, in so far as their writings condone such travesties, or in so far as they allow their analyses to be travestied without protesting. If the fashion is for communal authenticity, those anthropologists who would let it be understood, or who would themselves accept, that everything that is not western is or was communal, risk employing their 'scientific' authority to cover up one of the major intellectual mystifications of our times. Many writers and many different intellectual positions ought in this respect to be subjected to close scrutiny. This applies as much to Senghor as to Deleuze, and to all the meta-anthropological currents, that, paradoxically enough, celebrate difference and yet award the same encomium to all Stateless societies regardless; it should also be taken to include the diffuse ideologies of holiday clubs and local pottery sellers, not forgetting also the vague allusions of a Marxism that, since Marx, has grown a little weary of devoting itself to concrete social realities.

I hope that these remarks will not be misconstrued. The reaction of peoples who have suffered not merely ethnocide but also genocide is, when they are in a position to produce one, totally and absolutely justified. Besides, such events are a part of what is now happening. This is also the case with the regionalist demands that are, in a less tragic context, coming to light in Europe, and that have real causes and undeniable effects. It is nevertheless true (and therefore altogether urgent) that the 'here' that anthropologists ought to study is not a temporal 'elsewhere', a here that is the shadow of a merely fleeting presence and is therefore already absent. This ghostly silhouette is clearly still cast on *our* territories, distorting the view that *we* can have of them, but the use of the possessive and collective terms does again give rise to problems, since it refers artificially (and indiscriminately) to those who observe and to those that one observes, to anthropology and to its object. This remark corresponds to a traditional problem in anthropology: that of the relation between questioner and questioned, and of the objective situation that this relation creates.

If I regard 'modern' society of the western type as an object that can and must be studied, from the anthropological point of view, it is both because it offers a good vantage-point for observing the conjunction of relations of

force and relations of meaning, which is what an anthropological approach
should aim to do, and (complementing this) because it sheds new light on
the relation of the 'professional' observer to those around him – a relation
which has a direct effect on the production of anthropological 'knowledge'
and which is itself one of the constitutive aspects of relations of force. Some
interesting research along these lines has begun to develop in France, but so
far it is of experimental value only. I am thinking particularly of the research
in the areas of Paris and Nantes that Gerard Althabe has supervised. This
work has given rise to some very fruitful accounts and debates, to a series of
unfinished or unpublished texts and to a methodological account that was
summarised in a recent issue of *Dialectiques*.[2]

Gerard Althabe, whose research experience includes long periods spent
in black Africa and in Madagascar,[3] is primarily concerned to show how an
anthropological approach is applicable to the study of groups or institutions
that are characteristic of modern industrial society. Three key features are
taken by him to define the anthropological approach: it takes small-scale
social units as its object of investigation, by means of which it seeks to develop
an analysis that is of more general relevance, apprehending in some sense
the totality of the society into which it fits. This first characteristic corresponds to the double ambition that Lévi-Strauss attributes to anthropology
in *Structural Anthropology*. Second, given the obvious distance between
observer and observed, the anthropologist is, paradoxically enough, driven
to define an extreme (and often mythical) aim, for which he tries to supply
the methodological means, i.e., to elaborate 'the social science of the observed', as Lévi-Strauss puts it. Lastly (and this third feature is more particularly a part of Althabe's methodology, as elaborated in *Oppression et
libération dans l'imaginaire*), the relation established between the anthropologist and those who are the object of his enquiry conditions the sort of
knowledge to which he may have access. But, in the 'exotic' colonial or
post-colonial context, the anthropologist is not in control of this relation,
for two main reasons. First, this relation is to a large extent determined by a
total situation (in this context the role of the Europeans), and second, the
observer is unknowingly drawn into relations between subjects: a position
is assigned to him as an ideological actor in the debates, practices and relations that he seeks to 'observe'.

What happens to these features when anthropological enquiry takes place
in the modern western milieu, for example in the big urban agglomerations?
Anthropological investigations are then carried out in small and empirically
manageable units, such as stair-cases, blocks of flats, streets or cooperative
housing projects, for in places like this one can get some sense of the inhabitants' interpersonal relations. The methodology of such enquiries is central
to the anthropological approach, for the relation between the enquirer and
his subjects lasts a long time and is dependent on several factors. First, it is

determined by a total situation; the researchers (in this case, university intellectuals) are assigned places and statuses that are, by and large, a function of their class identity. This means both that one has to take account of the researchers' positions in order to read the interviews between researchers and 'researched', and also that the growing knowledge people have of the researchers' status has, in so far as it is a part of the relations studied, to be studied for its own sake. The relations between researchers and researched does, moreover, have a history: the interlocutors' respective positions develop, and this transformation has a direct effect on the production of knowledge.

The relations that have been uncovered clearly have to be placed in relation to the total socio-economic system; research into small living units or small-scale encounters makes it possible to construct a theory of interpersonal communication in clearly defined places, but the domain so defined is not an autonomous one. On the one hand, interpersonal communication is dependent on, or marked by, external codes and norms (the role of the media clearly springs to mind here); on the other hand, it is located in a space and a time that are defined, constructed and controlled by a system of total domination. All constraints linked to the organisation of space (for example, the distance between workplace and home) are quite obviously extraneous to the research itself. As Althabe so astutely observes, it would be as pointless to reduce the field of interpersonal communications to its external determinations as it would be to constitute it as an autonomous universe; the articulation of this field with these determinations is indeed the ultimate aim of such research.

It is clear that, in this type of research, the theme of personal communication is not exclusively nor principally psychological, but that through it one can take in at a glance the constitution of relations of meaning, by and for individuals, and their inscription in a social field with a multiplicity of dimensions and determinations. We are far from a social psychology that would be concerned with the difficulties and problems of adaptation of various social actors, a project in which social reality is always considered more or less as an intangible intellectual given, to which one was actually supposed to adapt, or in relation to which one was supposed to place oneself. The attempt to define a social logic is not, however, meant to imply that no total situation (as defined by precise socio-economic relations) exists, but rather that relations between individuals and relations to the institution are in some manner (itself the object of the analysis) the site where these general relations are apprehended, sometimes contested, but also, and in the last analysis, reproduced. This site has to do with symbolic efficacy, which cannot itself be dissociated from the relations of force that make up a society's empirical structure. I would argue that the analysis of social logic (or, if you like of the *ensemble* of particular social logics, as inscribed in various institutional frameworks, like kinship, residence, religion) is the actual object of anthropology, regardless of the diversity of historical, social or geographical milieux in which research unfolds.

Social logics

An anthropology of industrial societies would therefore depend on the same epistemological criteria and methodological constraints as affect all anthropological research. Here again we have to tackle the problem of the conceptual definition of the object, and if, more particularly, the institutional realities of our societies force us to return to this question, it is because the intellectual debate unfolding there does in fact bear on the status of that object, and because the manner in which one defines anthropology in modern societies necessarily presumes a definition of anthropology in general.

I have already had occasion to express my astonishment at the fact that some anthropologists could claim to wish for the death of anthropology. This is clearly only a figure of speech, but it testifies to a real confusion, as much in the formulation as in the underlying thought. Suppose we look at this question more closely. Economic anthropology that is Marxist in inspiration often tends to be quite disdainful in its attitude to anything that is not 'infrastructural', and anyone who ventures to suggest that the order of sociological and historical causes is not necessarily the same as the research into these causes risks being accused of idealism. After all, if one takes the metaphor of vertical instances literally, one can quite see that it is easier, both empirically and methodologically, to start with the more 'manifest' effects before proceeding to the 'deeper' causes, than to pursue the opposite course. So the tendency is for anthropologists to find it relatively easy to step over the symbolic apparatus in order to identify 'modes of production' directly, and then to find it even easier to unmask the pathetic screening effects of an ideology. Without wishing to disparage the shrewdness of the observers, one cannot help but wonder how on earth this ideology could have deceived the poor people who were being observed, and so effectively and for so long.

In the last analysis, the question raised by 'materialist' anthropologists (and the inverted commas are meant here not to dispute their right to this title, but to question their exclusive right to it) would run as follows: 'What is the point of refining the logic of kinship systems, of a corpus of myth or of ritual categories? What primarily interests us is the place that these realities occupy in a determinate social configuration, in the organisation of domination and in its reproduction.' Now, setting aside the difficulties peculiar to the notion of domination, it is surprising that it does not occur to the champions of sociologism and economism that there might be a link between the logic of thought, of action and of domination. This observation seems to me to apply not only to sociologism and economism, in that they eradicate every properly anthropological consideration from their analyses (i.e., every consideration of the functioning of the human mind or of the logic of symbolism) and from their treatment of the question of efficacy, but also to structuralism. For while structuralists claim to identify symbolic configurations and to uncover their logic (mytho-logics, for example), it does not occur to them that this logic can only be fully apprehended when operating 'beyond' these configurations, and that this is because they have eliminated every properly sociological consideration, and every reflection as to the nature of efficacy, from the anthropological framework.

A book like *La Révolution structurale*,[4] by Jean-Marie Benoist, is particularly illuminating here. We know that anthropological polemics lapse easily into a murderous tone, that some anthropologists want to kill anthropology whilst others saw in May '68 the death of structuralism. Benoist, however, is aware that Nietzsche has already tackled the death of God[5] and has therefore settled for killing Marx;[6] more recently, following Foucault, he would kill man as well. *Le Révolution structurale*, which is nevertheless a brilliant and informed book, represents a kind of breviary of 'theoretical anti-humanism' (to use Althusser's expression). It also defines structuralism as being, above all else, an anti-phenomenology, as being opposed to all philosophies of the subject, which is why it is relevant to my argument here.

Without going into details, I would admit that the convergence emphasised by Benoist between Althusser, Foucault, Pierre Nora and Jacques Le Goff, Chomsky, Lacan, the 'nouveau roman', Roland Barthes, Lévi-Strauss and several others seems to me to be a little forced, and that the 'subject' that their respective approaches place in question does not seem to me to be the same in every case. If, in particular, Lévi-Strauss actually does succeed in establishing the rules of the cultural unconscious (I have tried to demonstrate above that the category 'the unconscious' actually refers in his work to several different orders of reality), one of the most remarkable consequences of this theoretical advance lies in refusing to identify culture completely with society and in refusing to see society as a subject that would be expressed by its culture. The abandonment of culturalist reductivism is clearly not to be identified with a glorious defence of the universality of the categories of western reason, such as have been placed in question 'by the irruption of other logical forms, eastern or "primitive"' (Benoist), but it has even less to do with acknowledging the rise in Europe of an 'unreason' or 'irrationality' that psychoanalysis would show to be 'the break threatening western logic' and 'the irruption of the inner enemy, the great repressed of the history of metaphysics, i.e., the East'. Does this evocation of an East inside Europe amount to a return of the banished culturalist subject? In order to answer this question I would stress that it really is the culturalist subject that Lévi-Strauss eradicates or, at any rate, relativises, and this is how he manages to reveal the systems of transformation in which the temporary 'realisations' of cultures occur, systems whose existence alone gives a meaning to particular configurations.

The problem is indeed to define the level at which an analysis might succeed in showing how it is that the anthropological logic of the system is also the differential logic of the society, and how social logics simultaneously define the intellectual order and the social order, the anthropological dimension and the sociological dimension, the order of the symbolic and the order of ideology. In this respect, research devoted to thoroughly classical empirical objects, such as systems of descent and alliance, representations of the person, and ritual logic, are still quite topical and relevant. The still-to-be-shattered anthropological circle is the very one that refers us ineluctably from symbol to function or from evolution to culture, and vice versa; the substitution of sign for 'man', which Benoist sees as the essence and virtue of the 'structural revolution', may still be inscribed within this same circle and cannot therefore be said to shatter it. Benoist acknowledges the existence of a 'common ground' for the different 'semiotics' that constitute at the present moment the field of the human sciences (a semiotic of the unconscious (Lacan), a semiotic of kinship codes and of the corpus of myths (Lévi-Strauss), a semiotic of social relations and contradictions (Althusser), etc.), whilst at the same time admitting that these approaches are not to be confused with each other, and that their objects are mutually exclusive also. This 'common ground' is the *text* 'understood in a wide sense and therefore as transcending the limitations of the fabric of words in order to embrace all signifying systems and *ensembles*'. This text then becomes 'both the object of the enquiry and the place in which matters of epistemology are endlessly discussed, reformulated and redefined'.

But where anthropology is concerned, the notion of text is an ambiguous one. For it refers both to thought in a systematic sense (and here it only really exists in an unconscious form, i.e., as the total combinatory or as the whole system of transformations), and to discourses or practices that are, or could be, effected. In the latter case, it refers to a systematic notion of practice which only really exists in an implicit form, as the sum of what is possible and conceivable in a given society, where the society would have, moreover, to be considered as differential, as a function of the statuses that are inscribed in it. It seems to me that anthropologists need only concern themselves with the unconscious *qua* system when the full range of implicit practices is considered in its systematicity also. I would also argue that the latter cannot be defined without taking into account the diversity of speakers, the identity of the producers of signs, and those imprecise configurations in which tests of strength and trials of meaning are simultaneously at work – without, in short, reintroducing actors and subjects, and therefore historical production.

In other words, if anthropology, is to be revised it will be through struc-

110

turalism and Marxism, the two strong points in recent French anthropology. Structuralism is important not simply because structural analysis makes it possible to theorise the links between, and the respective weight of, symbolic systems that hitherto had been treated as isolated (a form of analysis which, let me repeat, always to some degree refers to a highly mechanistic conception of superimposed instances), but rather because it brings to light logics governing practice which allow one to qualify the previous epistemological divisions and to dispense with the allied conception of layered systems.[7] I refer to Marxism here because Marxist analysis makes it possible to re-place a language of instances and a functionalist language (which sometimes serves to refine the former) with an anthropological analysis of the effects of domination and of symbolic efficacy. One then has to decide whether the contributions of the other human sciences are necessary for a revision of this sort.

A myth, a necessity: interdisciplinarity

I do not propose to tackle every aspect of interdisciplinarity here, but will simply show how anthropological researchers have to confront this problem nowadays. We know how Lévi-Strauss drew his inspiration for his anthro-pological models from structural linguistics, and how French anthropology thus enjoyed a theoretical revival. I have already suggested (and it is a com-mon, even trivial, and possibly excessively hasty remark) that one risks losing on the historical side of things what one has gained in overall cogency. This failing in structuralist thinking has been denounced by those favouring a 'dynamic' approach, and by the Marxists, but it is perhaps Bourdieu who has provided the most astute assessment of it. He identifies in it one of those logical alternatives (the contradictory need to study symbolic thought as both 'structured' and 'structuring') that define two of the constitutive points of what I have called the anthropological circle.

Nowadays the notion of interdisciplinarity may be taken to tally fairly exactly with the areas in which each discipline is incomplete and lacking in confidence, and it may therefore be said to be at the cross-roads of intel-lectual confusions. Intedisciplinarity is the proud title we give to the anxiety from which the different disciplines suffer; but this anxiety is in itself healthy, for whilst no-one any longer takes the notion seriously (there was a heroic period during which 'couples' from different disciplines, i.e., an ethnologist and a geographer, would set out for Africa, and would clearly be expected to cover the whole of the social field with more ease than if they had worked on their own), everyone has become far more attentive to the reality that corresponds with it.

Anthropologists and psychoanalysts are still, in spite of a long history of mutual curiosity and irritation, and of particular contributions bearing on

111

the question,[8] swopping visiting cards, but are no nearer to uniting their respective destinies. Alfred Adler has weighed up this mutual incomprehension,[9] and has blamed it on the dogmatism of the psychoanalysts. The only 'debate' between the two disciplines is still that bearing on the universality or non-universality of the Oedipus complex, but so long as it is formulated in these terms it is quite certain that no new anthropological definitions or projects will emerge. But I also believe that those intelligent enough to adopt a different approach in their treatment of the realities with which ethnology and psychoanalysis have to deal (and I am thinking of Deleuze and Guattari, in particular) have actually constructed a philosophical system whose imperatives reduce anthropological data, rather than a model that would enable them to understand both ethnological and analytic contributions. It is true, however, that generations of researchers have returned from the 'field' with an immense wealth of knowledge, as much in the domain of myth as in that of ritual. The idea is gradually emerging that every theory of power is inseparable from a theory of the person and from reflections as to the nature of death;[10] in this respect, it is not so much that psychoanalysis and anthropology share a common theoretical mode of enquiry but rather that their empirical curiosities converge, and that they are therefore obliged, come what may, to arrive at a kind of agreement.

Things are not the same with history and anthropology. Each discipline has felt and admitted a need for the other, although they should not, to my mind, ever be totally confused. Their methods and objects differ to the degree that some of the domains that the historian investigates (price changes, state of the world market, demographic changes) do, by their very nature, elude an anthropological approach. But anthropologists have discovered that the societies they study have a history just when historians, along with Fernand Braudel, were discovering the structural dimension of historical 'long time' (*longue durée*). Jacques le Goff[11] notes that history, as a science of how societies change, is tending rather to become a history of everyday life, a history of the depths and of 'mentalities', which both draws its inspiration from developments in psychoanalysis (particularly in the work of authors like Alain Besançon or Michel de Certeau) and also latches on to objects that are traditionally thought of as anthropological (like myth, women, childhood, death, etc.). One ought also to mention the attempts of certain historians to write genuine ethnological monographs, the most remarkable example so far being *Montaillou*, by Emmanuel le Roy Ladurie.[12]

It is not certain, however, that anyone has yet clearly defined the conditions for the new discipline of 'historical anthropology', whose object would be defined in terms of an ever-deeper insight into the nature of the respective objects of the two previously distinct disciplines. In fact, anthropologists feel, along with the need to think about periods of transition and about the institutions which express and produce change, the parallel need to give some theoretical status to phenomena that are too hastily termed 'marginal'; in short, to develop a systematic account of transition and of practice. This is occurring at a time when historians, conscious of permanent features, of recurrences and of the total social fact, have ceased to feel hostile towards synchronic studies, although still wary of the dangers they entail.

These approaches, although in some sense the inverse of each other, undoubtedly represent the same need – that of apprehending, alongside quantitative and functional assessments of facts and of changes, the less immediate reasons for permanent features, for possible tensions and discontinuities, for order and for its subversion. There are no 'infrastructural' changes that are not, in certain respects, the products of an action and the objects of an interpretation, i.e., the sites of a symbolic efficacy. Were anthropologists to forget, historians would always be ready to remind them that symbolic systems are not destined simply to be read and deciphered, and that their logic is that of a practice.[13] Anthropologists, on the other hand, might sometimes remind historians that the nature of the phenomena they are describing is more problematic (and therefore more important) than they seem to believe. I am thinking, for instance, of phenomena like 'witchcraft', and of the fact that a reading of the work of certain historians (like Le Roy Ladurie in *Les Paysans du Languedoc*)[14] does not make it clear whether they are referring to beliefs or to practices. Whilst it would clearly be out of the question to deny that every belief gives rise to a number of corresponding practices, or that it may entail a shift into action, it is by no means irrelevant to try and find out if these beliefs are or are not primary and inaugural. Thus, I would argue that witchcraft belief is a confirmation of the more general system (no devil without God), whereas an emphasis on the actual practices tends to give the impression that it is, as Michelet had argued, a manifestation of opposition to, and protest against, the established order. If the reality or unreality of the witches' sabbath is considered a trivial or insoluble question, the whole problematic of domination and of ideology is swept under the carpet. Historians cannot help but find suggestive parallels in the anthropological literature, not because the phenomena concerned are strictly identical or comparable with those that they study themselves, but because it offers a more systematic approach to the sort of intellectual problems to which the definition of this type of phenomenon gives rise.

But it is nonetheless true that anthropologists have felt a real need to write history. Africanists like Emmanuel Terray spring to mind here, for it is impossible for them to grasp the political reality of the societies they study without reconstructing them in a very literal way. The same is true of writers like Claude-Hélène Perrot or Claude Tardits, and it is genuinely hard to decide whether their efforts to define the logic of the political system through oral traditions qualify as anthropological or as historical. The work of a historian like Nathan Wachtel[15] shows the advantages of writing a retrospective history whose point of departure is the structural analysis of villages that he is studying now. Everyone has recourse to several different methods, and in this sense it might be argued that the best interdisciplinarity is the one that each is anyway practising on his own; but it is also the case that historians and anthropologists increasingly acknowledge that they are investigating the same empirical objects, and they are therefore increasingly aware of the need to construct and to investigate the same intellectual configurations.[16]

The most recent dialogue concerns social anthropology, biology, and the most innovatory aspects of physical anthropology, and clearly we have witnessed so far only the first tentative attempts to reconcile these conflicting disciplines. But it is one thing to allow that, in the end (an end that is not yet in sight), we will be able to discern convergences and correspondences between biological order and social order, it is quite another to accept the value of comparing the analytic methods proper to these different disciplines, and yet another (and a far more precarious position at that) to consider substituting a natural history of man for anthropology and history. I do not dispute the scope and intelligence of Edgar Morin's works, but there seems to be no place in them for a properly sociological apprehension of the facts; they base their analysis of the species on elements which are not, in themselves, problematic, but which, where the analysis of social groups is concerned, represent an area where there is maximal conflict over definition of terms. Once one has taken individual and society as the basic elements for one's theory, entities that are both phantastical and intellectually obvious, it is no problem at all to stage the few acts of the historical drama that are presumed to effect our passage from the archaic society to the State–town; and once one has referred to belief and religion as if they were obvious notions, their effects become equally self-evident (why be surprised if where there's smoke there's fire?). Alienation, domination and repression are likewise identified, measured and dated, but in no case do they have to be analysed or investigated. When one finds a writer like Jacques Ruffié[17] quite happily identifying ideology with learned culture, and what is more, considering the courtly literature of the eleventh and twelfth centuries as a resurgence of the old Neolithic and 'matriarchal' heritage, one can rest assured that analysis has a real contribution to make, in that it can replace such overblown notions with the study of social and cultural facts.

But in any case the anthropologist may protest and assert that, in its concern to question its own use of concepts and notions, as in its consciousness of constructing intellectual objects that are clearly and rigorously linked to the empirical materials that it observes, anthropology is far more scientific, and at any rate, far more serious than people who are not primarily engaged in it would imagine. This 'I am not what you think' may well have the virtue of modifying any premature assumptions as to the state of communication between disciplines and, thereby, may help to guarantee their future. For it is quite true that the human sciences, in the widest sense of the term, would have no meaning if they did not allow as a distant aim (which is also their whole justification) the identity of their project with their object.

Notes

Introduction

1 The following books, in particular, come to mind: E. E. Evans-Pritchard, *Social Anthropology* (London, 1967); R. Lowie, *The History of Ethnological Theory* (New York, 1938); P. Mercier, *Histoire de l'anthropologie* (Paris, 1966). On more specific topics one should consult: G. Balandier, *Political Anthropology*, translated by A. M. Sheridan (London, 1972); J. Lombard, *L'Anthropologie britannique contemporaine* (Paris, 1972).
2 C. Lévi-Strauss, *Structural Anthropology*, translated by C. Jakobson and B. G. Schoepf (London, 1968).
3 The expression 'vision of the defeated' is taken from the title of Nathan Wachtel's latest work, *La Vision des vaincus* (Paris, 1971).
4 J. Rancière, *La Leçon d'Althusser* (Paris, 1974).
5 H. Clastres, 'Les beaux-frères ennemis. A propos du cannibalisme Tupinamba' in *Nouvelle Revue de Psychanalyse*, 6 (Autumn, 1972).
6 See for instance the very interesting book edited by Rayna R. Reiter, *Toward an Anthropology of Women* (New York and London, 1975).

1. The anthropological circle

1 J. Rancière, *La Leçon d'Althusser*.
2 E. Terray, *Marxism and 'Primitive' Societies: Two Studies*, translated by Mary Klopper (New York and London, 1972).
3 M. Panoff, *Ethnologie: le deuxième souffle* (Paris, 1977).
4 R. Lowie, *The History of Ethnological Theory*.
5 These six types derive from Murdock's classification. G. P. Murdock, *Social Structure* (New York, 1949); *Outline of World Cultures*, Human Relations Area File (New Haven, 1963).
6 A group comprising all the descendants in the agnatic line (patriclan) or uterine line (matriclan) of the same ancestor.
7 A set of behaviours and rituals through which the husband, at the birth of one of his children, plays the social and physiological role of the mother.
8 R. Establet, 'Culture et idéologie' in *Cahiers Marxistes-Léninistes*, 12–13 (June–October, 1966).
9 See for instance G. Devereux, *Ethnopsychoanalysis: Psychoanalysis and Anthropology as Complementary Frames of Reference* (Berkeley, 1978).
10 Association of an animal or vegetable spirit with a human group (clan, lineage, moiety) or, sometimes, with a man.

116

NOTE

11 C. Lévi-Strauss, *Totemism*, translated by R. Needham (London, 1967).

12 E. R. Leach, *Rethinking Anthropology* (London, 1961).

13 C. Meillassoux, *Anthropologie économique des Gouro de Côte-d'Ivoire. De l'économie de subsistance à l'agriculture commerciale* (Paris, 1964).

14 E. Terray, *Marxism and 'Primitive' Societies*.

15 I have Lévi-Strauss's *Mythologies* in mind here and, as far as stories are concerned, the examples treated by Denise Paulme in *La Mère dévorante* (Paris, 1977).

16 L. Dumont, *From Mandeville to Marx. The Genesis and Triumph of Economic Ideology*, Chicago, 1977, the French version of which appeared as *Homo aequalis. Genèse et épanouissement de l'idéologie économique*, (Paris, 1977).

17 L. Dumont, *Homo Hierarchicus: the Caste System and its Implications*, translated by Mark Sainsbury (London, 1970).

18 E. Morin, *Le Paradigme perdu: la nature humaine* (Paris, 1973).

19 G. Balandier, *Political Anthropology*.

20 One can find an inkling of this sort of enquiry both in the work of a philosopher like Castoriadis (in the notion of 'social imaginary' that is expounded in *L'Institution imaginaire de la société*, Paris, 1975) and in the work of an anthropologist like Godelier who is trying at the moment to work out the place of the 'ideal' in the 'real'. The reader could also consult some of my own studies, and in particular the Introduction to *L'Anthropologie religieuse* (Paris, 1974), *Théorie des pouvoirs et idéologie* (Paris, 1975), and *Pouvoirs de vie, pouvoirs de mort* (Paris, 1977).

21 More particularly, several works by John Middleton.

22 H. Hubert and M. Mauss, 'L'esquisse d'une théorie générale de la magie' in *L'Année Sociologique* (1904).

23 See, in particular, *The Sexual Life of Savages in North-Western Melanesia* (London, 1929), *Sex and Repression in Savage Society* (London, 1927), *Argonauts of the Western Pacific* (London, 1922), *Coral Gardens and their Magic*, 2 vols (London, 1935).

24 Malinowski's influence on American psycho-dynamic theory (and on Kardiner, in particular) is clear enough, and has been acknowledged as such. Whilst the definition of a 'basic personality' is very closely linked to all the tenets of the American culturalist school, the definition of an institution as a relation set up between the individual and his environment and the distinction between primary and secondary institutions are very close to those of Malinowski. Consult, in this respect, A. Kardiner and E. Preble, *They Studied Man* (London, 1962).

25 A. Kardiner and E. Preble, *They Studied Man*. Ruth Benedict highlights the finished character of each 'cultural configuration' (see for instance *Patterns of Culture*, New York, 1935) whilst Margaret Mead studies the coherence of the relations between cultural *patterns* and *patterns* of individual conduct. These formulations predate the notion of 'basic personality' that the American psycho-dynamic school had proposed, and to which I have referred above.

26 M. Griaule, *Masques dogons* (Paris, 1938); M. Griaule, *Conversations with Ogotomeli*, translated by Ralph Butler, revised by A. I. Richards and B. Hooke (London, 1965); G. Dieterlen, *Essai sur la religion bambara* (Paris, 1951); D. Zahan, *Sociétés d'initiation bambara, le n'domo, le koré* (Paris, 1960).

27 A. Adler, 'Avunculat et mariage matrilatéral en Afrique Noire' and Luc de Heusch, 'Parenté et histoire en Afrique Centrale (réponse à Alfred Adler)' both in *L'Homme*, XVI, 4 (1976).

28 A. Adler and M. Cartry, 'La transgression et sa dérision' in *L'Homme*, XI, 3 (1971).

29 Cf. J. Laplanche and J.-B. Pontalis, 'Oedipus complex' in *The Language of Psychoanalysis*, translated by Donald Nicholson (London, 1973) and C. Backès-Clément's commentaries in *L'Anthropologie: science des sociétés primitives* (Paris, 1971).

30 R. Girard, *Violence and the Sacred*, translated by Patrick Gregory (Baltimore, 1977).
31 C. Backès-Clément, *L'Anthropologie*.
32 *Le Monde*, 28 July 1977.

2. Some questions concerning the current state of anthropology

1 G. Deleuze and F. Guattari, *Anti-Oedipus*, translated by R. Hurley, M. Seen and H. R. Lane (New York, 1977).
2 C. Castoriadis, *L'Institution imaginaire de la société* (Paris, 1975).
3 Malinowski, 'Anthropology', in *Encyclopedia Britannica*, suppl. vol. I (New York and London, 1936).
4 Reprinted in *L'Institution imaginaire de la société*.
5 C. Lévi-Strauss, *The Raw and the Cooked, Introduction to a Science of Mythology*, I, translated by John and Doreen Weightman (London, 1964), translation modified.
6 'Genèse et structure du champ religieux' in *Revue Française de Sociologie*, XII (1971).
7 'If one is always justified in leaving to one side, at least provisionally, the question of the economic and social functions of mythical, ritual or religious systems that are subjected to analysis, in as much as, calling an interpretation "allegorical" they act as an obstacle to structural interpretation, the fact remains that this methodological division becomes increasingly sterile and dangerous as one moves away from the symbolic productions of the less-differentiated societies or from the less-differentiated symbolic productions (such as language, the product of the anonymous and collective labour of successive generations) of societies divided into classes.'
8 *Outline of a Theory of Practice*, translated by Richard Nice (Cambridge, 1974).
9 D. Sperber, *Rethinking Symbolism*, translated by A. L. Morton (Cambridge, 1975).
10 N. Chomsky, 'The general properties of language' in I. L. Darley (ed.), *Brain Mechanisms underlying Speech and Language* (New York and London, 1967).
11 I could also have mentioned the problems of 'writers' block', a phenomenon that is familiar enough to most of us and is not so much a question of relative ease of writing as of the courage to advance fairly wide-ranging interpretations. Those so inspired (in recent years, Maurice Godelier and Claude Meillassoux) are setting themselves up as targets and therefore have to have strong nerves. This aside, which is not meant as just a token gesture, will, I hope, serve to provide a context for the more virulent critiques formulated in the present work.
12 Beside the books considered here, I would also cite (with no pretence to being exhaustive) Meyer Fortes and Jack Goody, for their theories of the lineage, of descent and of alliance, Edmund Leach and Rodney Needham for their discussions of structuralism, and Jack Middleton for his analysis of religious facts.
13 Cf. Jack Goody, *Production and Reproduction, a Comparative Study of the Domestic Domain* (Cambridge, 1976).
14 Marshall Sahlins, *Culture and Practical Reason* (Chicago, 1967).
15 Rodney Needham provides a particularly striking example of a hyper-theoretical anti-theoretician (a paradox which doubtless helps to explain his changing attitudes to structuralism). In his contributions to *Rethinking Kinship and Marriage*, ed. R. Needham (London, 1971) he emphasises the danger of 'prematurely erecting a grandiose theory', evokes the failure of Radcliffe-Brown and Lévi-Strauss and quite properly insists on the need for in-depth case studies, but his real theoretical ambition comes to light when he suggests quite simply that all the categories employed in anthropological analysis are false ones: 'The intention behind these remarks has been to argue that anthropological research has been misguided, in even the supposedly basic topics of kinship and marriage, by certain conceptual failings.' What Needham

118

is here proposing (like Leach, in his discussion of the notions of unilineal descent and complementary filiation) is a conceptual reorganisation resulting in the constitution of new intellectual objects. Taking his inspiration from Wittgenstein, he denounces 'the tendency to look for something in common to all the entities we commonly subsume under a general term', and he suggests that modes of descent, forms of marriage, kinship terminologies and incest prohibitions constitute, each in their way, *ensembles* which may have elements in common but are not defined by essential and characteristic features. Thus, the contractual union could be the sole feature common to diverse forms of marriage, and incest prohibitions could have nothing in common with each other, except prohibition – which would imply that the rules concerning incest in diverse societies are not necessarily comparable.

Every reorganisation of the intellectual domain is in itself stimulating, and I would await with curiosity and impatience the positive and systematic results of Needham's arguments, if I did not fear that, as is sometimes the case with Leach, he displays more intuition than perseverance and startles hares that are just too quick for him.

16 I do not therefore mean to disparage an author like Luc de Heusch (*Essais sur le symbolisme de l'inceste royal en Afrique*, Solvay, 1958; *Why marry her? Society and Symbolic Structures* translated by Janet Lloyd (Cambridge, 1981). I would also recommend Jean Pouillon's structuralist articles (most of which are assembled in *Fétiches sans fétichisme*, Paris, 1975) and those of Edmund Leach's writings, subsequently qualified, if not repudiated, in which he adopts a structuralist approach (see his *Lévi-Strauss*, London, 1971).

17 These writers are so disparate that it is impossible to talk of a school or of a group; but some collective works (*Le Développement du commerce en Afrique Noire*, Oxford, 1971; *L'Esclavage en Afrique Noire*, Paris, 1975) and polemical writings testify to the existence and vitality of this theoretical current. There are anthropologists (like Maurice Bloch in England), or historians (most obviously, the young historians working with the Africanist Ivor Wilks in the United States), in England and the United States who are interested in this development, or have been influenced by it.

18 'Race and History', reprinted in *Structural Anthropology*, II.

19 See 'Race and History': 'The notion of a biological evolution corresponds to a hypothesis to which has been attributed the highest coefficient of probability found in the natural sciences. On the other hand, the notion of a social or cultural evolution only contributes at the most an attractive but dangerously convenient means of presentation of the facts.'

20 J. Pouillon, Afterword to the French edition of *Race et histoire* (Paris, 1961), entitled 'L'œuvre de Claude Lévi-Strauss'.

21 C. Lévi-Strauss, *Tristes Tropiques*, translated by John and Doreen Weightman (London, 1973).

22 C. Lévi-Strauss, 'Language and the analysis of social laws' in *Structural Anthropology*.

23 J. Pouillon, Afterword to *Race et histoire*.

24 C. Lévi-Strauss, *The Elementary Structures of Kinship*, translated by J. H. Bell and J. R. von Stürmer, and edited by R. Needham (London, 1968).

25 *Ibid.*

26 The three elementary structures of exchange (bilateral, matrilateral, patrilateral) 'are always present in the human mind, at any rate in an unconscious form, and . . . it cannot evoke one of them without thinking it as being opposed to, but also correlated with, the two others', C. Lévi-Strauss, *ibid.*

27 In a harmonic regime residence rules and descent rules are in 'harmony' – for instance, patrilineal descent and parilocality or matrilineal descent and avunculocality

are characteristic of harmonic regimes, whereas a matrilineal society in which the son lives with his father will be termed disharmonic.

28 *Tristes Tropiques.*
29 In M. Mauss, *Sociologie et anthropologie* (Paris, 1950).
30 See the chapters in *Structural Anthropology* entitled 'The sorcerer and his magic' and 'The efficacy of symbols'.
31 See *L'Homme*, xv, 3–4 (1975).
32 E. R. Leach, 'Rethinking anthropology', chapter 1 on *Rethinking Anthropology*.
33 I have given a fuller account of Leach's arguments in *La Construction du monde* and *Les Domaines de la parenté* (both edited by M. Augé, Paris, 1974 and 1975).
34 Along with Barnes, Mitchell, Van Velsen and Middleton. Here one should consult Lombard's *L'Anthropologie britannique contemporaine*, particularly pages 209 and 210, where he recalls the opposition that Gluckman had himself (with Eggan) formulated in the introduction to *Political Systems and the Distribution of Power* (London, 1965), between a line featuring himself, Fortes and Goody, and another line, featuring Lévi-Strauss, Leach and Needham. The first line favoured theories of descent and empirical models, the second placed its emphasis on alliance and on the models as constructed by the anthropologist.
35 V. W. Turner, *Schism and Continuity in Tribal Africa* (Manchester, 1957); *The Forest of Symbols: Aspects of Ndembu Rituals* (New York, 1967); *The Ritual Process, Structure and Anti-Structure* (London, 1969).
36 M. Eliade, *Rites and Symbols of Initiation* (New York, 1965).
37 I am thinking here of Nadel (*The Nuba*, London and New York, 1947; *Nupe Religion*, London, 1954), who was interested in both rites of passage and transvestism, and of Gluckman's studies of the Zulus and the Wiko.
38 In his contribution to two collective works, J. Roux (ed.) *Questions à la sociologie française* (Paris, 1976) and F. Pouillon (ed.) *L'Anthropologie économique* (Paris, 1976).
39 Documentation and detailed analyses dealing with all of these questions may be found in the collective work cited above, *L'Anthropologie économique.* The reader might also care to look at two monographs, *Anthropologie économique des Gouro de Côte-d'Ivoire. De l'économie de subsistance à l'agriculture commerciale*, by Claude Meillassoux, and *Les Dida de Côte-d'Ivoire*, by Emmanuel Terray, and two collective works, edited by Meillassoux, *The Development of Indigenous Trade and Markets in West Africa. L'évolution du commerce africain depuis le XIXe Siècle en Afrique de l'Ouest* (London, 1971) and *L'Esclavage en Afrique précoloniale: Dix-sept études* (Paris, 1975).
40 F. Pouillon, in *L'Anthropologie économique.*
41 More particularly in his last work, *Maidens' Meal and Money. Capitalism and the Domestic Community* (Cambridge 1981).
42 M. Godelier, 'Mode de production, rapports de parenté et structures démographiques' in *La Pensée*, 172 (1973).
43 F. Pouillon, in *L'Anthropologie économique.*
44 Maurice Godelier is quite definite about this, and in agreement with Lévi-Strauss – at least in the interview published in *L'Homme*, xv, 3–4, (1975). 'Anthropologie, histoire, idéologie', between Claude Lévi-Strauss, Marc Augé and Maurice Godelier, and translated as 'Anthropology, history, ideology', in *Critique of Anthropology*, 2, 6 (1976).
45 P. P. Rey, *Colonialisme, néo-colonialisme et transition au capitalisme. Exemple de la 'Comilog' au Congo-Brazzaville* (Paris, 1971).
46 E. Terray, *Marxism and 'Primitive' Societies: Two Studies*, translated by Mary Klopper (New York and London, 1972).

47 M. Godelier (in collaboration with José Garanger) 'Outils de pierre, outils d'acier chez les Baruya de Nouvelle-Guinée', in *L'Homme*, XIII, 3 (1973).
48 P. P. Rey, *Colonialisme, néo-colonialisme et transition au capitalisme*.
49 M. Godelier (in collaboration with José Garanger), 'Outils de pierre, outils d'acier'.
50 The extent of the misunderstanding may be gauged by referring to these remarks by Lévi-Strauss in 'Race and History': 'In everything which concerns family organisation and the harmonious relationships between familial and social groups, the Australians, who are backward on the economic level, are so far ahead of the rest of humanity that it is necessary, in order to understand the systems of rules they elaborated in a conscious and thoughtful manner, to call upon the most sophisticated forms of modern mathematics . . . The articulation of families through intermarriages may lead to the formation of broad bonds between a few entities or of small bonds between numerous groupings; but, small or large, it is these hinges which keep the whole social structure together and give it its flexibility. In a manner often very lucid, the Australians have made up the theory of this mechanism and listed the principal methods which make it possible, with the advantages and disadvantages of each. They have thus gone beyond the level of empirical observation and proceeded to the knowledge of certain laws regulating the system' (p. 343, translation modified).
51 It seems that in ancient Egypt only the 'pharaonic' model of brother–sister incest was extended to a section of ordinary society. Lévi-Strauss draws attention to this fact but it may actually be a question of a secondary phenomenon whose incidence is anyway little known. The book by Luc de Heusch cited above may usefully be consulted on the question of royal incest in East Africa, and on the relations between incest and power, cf. Marc Augé, *Pouvoirs de vie, pouvoirs de mort. Introduction à une anthropologie de la répression* (Paris, 1978).
52 The resulting distinction in so-called lineage societies, between a 'tribal-village' system and a 'lineage' system seems to me to be doubtful from the sociological point of view. The study of societies with lineages and age classes (i.e., village systems) in Africa would seem, on the contrary, to indicate that it is impossible to analyse the one without the other (in as much as one wishes to account for actual functioning), or more exactly, that lineages and age classes together make up a system. It goes without saying, moreover, that every interpretation of the two institutions in terms of historical succession, followed by coexistence, would be quite unwarranted.
53 Causality of the different 'instances' in their internal effects on each other, as analysed by Godelier in *Horizon, trajets Marxistes en anthropologie* (Paris, 1973).
54 M. Godelier, Preface to *Sur les sociétés précapitalistes. Textes choisis de Marx, Engels, Lénine* (Paris, 1970).
55 M. Godelier, *Horizon, trajets Marxistes en anthropologie*.
56 A. Marie, 'Rapports de parenté et rapports de production dans les sociétés lignagères' in F. Pouillon (ed.), *L'Anthropologie économique*.
57 L. Sebag, *Marxisme et structuralisme* (Paris, 1967).

3. From moral crisis to intellectual doubt

1 J. Copans, 'Anthropologie et impérialisme', in *Les Temps Modernes*, 293–4, December 1970–January 1971 and 299–300, July–August, 1971; *Anthropologie et impérialisme, textes choisis et présentés par Jean Copans* (Paris, 1975).
2 J. Copans, *Critiques et politiques de l'anthropologie* (Paris, 1974). Cf. also *Le Mal de voir* (Paris, 1976), a work in which Henri Moniot has assembled most of the contributions made at two conferences on 'Orientalisme, africanisme, américanisme'

(9–11 May 1974) and on 'Ethnologie et politique au Maghreb' (5 June 1975). I have in mind various articles by George Condominas and by Jean Pouillon. Denunciations of ethnocide (Robert Jaulin) are phenomena of a different order.
3 Nos 84–5, October–November, 1952.
4 S. Adotévi, *Négritude et négrologues* (Paris, 1972).
5 P. Hountondji, *Sur la 'philosophie' africaine* (Paris, 1976).
6 P. Tempels, *Bantoe-Filosefie*, Antwerp, 1946. Hountondji points out in a note that this text had first been translated (into French) in 1945 and published by Lovania Editions at Elisabethville (now Lubumbashi), before being edited by Présence Africaine in 1949, and the Présence Africaine edition is now in its third reprinting.
7 'A vague system of thought that stems from Aristotle's philosophy, from Christian theology and from raw common sense', as Hountondji puts it in a footnote.
8 D. Zahan, *Sociétés d'initiation bambara, le n'domo, le koré* (Paris, 1960).
9 Louis-Vincent Thomas, *Les Diola. Essai d'analyse fonctionnelle sur une population de Basse Casamance* (Dakar, 1959).
10 Alexis Kagame, *La Philosophie bantu-rwandaise de l'etre* (Brussels, 1956).
11 A. Makaraziza, *La Dialectique des Barundi* (Brussels, 1959).
12 V. Mulago, *Un Visage africain du christianisme* (Paris, 1965).
13 L. S. Senghor, *Nation et voie africaine du socialisme* (Paris, 1964).
14 A. Adesanya, 'Yoruba metaphysical thinking', in *Odu*, 5 (1958).
15 In spite of his respect for Nkrumah, Hountondji is not too keen on his *Consciencisme.* cf. *Philosophy and Ideology for Decolonisation with Particular Reference to the African Revolution* (London, 1964).
16 A. Césaire, *Discourse on Colonialism*, translated by John Pinkham (New York and London, 1972), translations modified.
17 See in particular, *La Paix blanche* (Paris, 1970); *Gens de soi, gens de l'autre* (Paris, 1973).
18 See in particular, *Chronique des Indiens Guyaki* (Paris, 1972); *Society Against the State*, translated by Robert Hurley (New York, 1977). I wrote the above lines before the tragic death of Pierre Clastres. I have decided on reflection, that to tone down the slightly aggressive quality of certain expressions would not be a proper homage to pay to his talent as an ethnographer, and to the vigour, itself sometimes too polemical, of his thought.
19 J. Baudrillard, *Le Miroir de la production* (Paris, 1973).
20 I would add here that my choice of terms is not crucial and that one could equally well keep the term 'sociology', thus remaining faithful to the Durkheimian tradition, and to the kind of approach that, over and above actual diversity, tends to aim at grasping totalities and generalities.
21 R. Bastide, *Anthropologie appliquée* (Paris, 1971).
22 This commentary is reprinted in *Anthropologie et impérialisme* (Paris, 1975) and derives from a talk given at a conference at the Seminario de Estudios Antropológicos held at the Instituto Indigenista Interamericano de México. Alfonso Villa Rojas's article is entitled 'En torno a la nueva tendencia ideológica de antropólogos e indigenistas', or 'Regarding the new ideological tendency among anthropologists and those concerned with "ethnic" politics', in *América Indígena*, XXIX, 3 (July, 1969).
23 A distinction introduced by Hans Reichenbach in *Experience and Prediction* (Chicago, 1961).
24 Gérard Leclerc has pursued some very interesting lines of thought on this subject in *Anthropologie et colonialisme* (Paris, 1972).
25 Certain researchers, not all of whom were anthropologists, denounced the biased or simply erroneous interpretations that the media were offering of the drought and

famine in the Sahel, and their contribution seems to me to correspond very exactly to what critical research ought to be capable of achieving. Cf. Comité Information Sahel, *Qui se nourrit de la famine en Afrique? Le dossier politique de la famine au Sahel* (Paris, 1974).

26 R. Buijtenhuijs, 'L'Anthropologie révolutionnaire; comment faire?' in *Anthropologie et impérialisme.*

27 K. Gough, 'Des propositions nouvelles pour les anthropologues', in *Anthropologie et impérialisme*, first published as 'New proposals for anthropologists', in *Current Anthropology*, ix, 5 (1968).

28 This is the title of an article by Yves Lacoste ('La géographie, ça sert à faire la guerre') in the extremely interesting review, *Herodote* (Paris, 1976).

29 Which does not mean, indeed quite the contrary (as the reader will have grasped), that the groups and situations brought to light in the present conjuncture do not constitute empirical points of departure for a deepening or a recasting of theoretical anthropology.

30 'Le rouge et le noir', in *Anthropologie et impérialisme.*

Conclusions

1 Which, it is worth noting, has for some time been getting a bad press; popular songs prefer to celebrate the 'chouans', which are models of egalitarian anti-Jacobinism.

2 'Le quotidien en procès', interview in *Dialectiques*, 21 (1977).

3 See in particular *Oppression et libération dans l'imaginaire* (Paris, 1969).

4 Paris, 1975.

5 It is worth noting that God, as, almost by definition, is His habit, is coming back into favour today, as much with the so-called 'new' philosophers as with the 'regionalisms' (the celebration of Mass in Corsican, for instance, draws up the battle-lines where they were least expected). One cannot rule out the possibility that those Catholic integrationalists who are still occupying Saint-Nicholas-du-Chardonnett will soon assume the quality of old Indians.

6 J. M. Benoist, *Marx est mort* (Paris, 1970).

7 Françoise Héritier's works are a perfect example of this.

8 I have Gezà Roheim in mind here.

9 A. Adler, 'Totem sans tabou', in *Nouvelles Littéraires*, 2559, 18–24 November, 1976, in the dossier 'Anthropologie ambiguë', assembled by George Balandier.

10 The originality of Louis-Vincent Thomas's latest work is worth noting here.

11 I am thinking in particular of his article 'L'anthropologie au rendez-vous de l'histoire' in the issue of *Nouvelles Littéraires* mentioned in n.9 above.

12 Translated by Barbara Bravy (New York and London, 1978).

13 Jacques le Goff (in 'Les gestes symboliques dans la vie sociale. Les gestes de la vassalité', Settimane di studio del Centro Italiano di stuli sull'alto medioevo, XXIII Simboli e Simbologie nell' Alto Medioevo, Spoleto, 3–9 April 1975, Spoleto, 1976) demonstrates the logic of a symbolic system in which the tie of fealty (homage and faith) linked to the investiture of a fief depends on the tie of vassality. This text has been republished in *Pour un autre Moyen Age* (Paris, 1977).

14 Paris, 1966.

15 N. Wachtel, *Les Visions des vaincus.*

16 A young review like *Espace Temps* bears out this need.

17 Given the importance of Ruffié's works, his hasty ventures in the field of anthropological synthesis are all the more disappointing, e.g., Bernard J. Ruffié, 'Hématologie et culture', in *Les Annales*, July–August, 1976.

123

Index

Adesanya, A., 85
Adler, A., 39, 112, 117n.27
Adotévi, S., 82, 92
Africa, 2, 9, 46, 48, 64, 79, 82–6, 106
age-classes, 64
alienation, 43, 45
Althabe, G., 106, 107
Althusser, L., 5, 6, 15, 30, 31, 66, 71, 74–6,
    109, 110
Amin, S., 66
Ancient Society, 19
L'Anthropologie britannique contemporaine,
    61
Anthropologie et impérialisme, 99
anthropologists
    American, 96, 99
    English-speaking, vii, 7, 32, 48, 64, 79
    French-speaking, vii, 3, 7, 37, 48, 79, 99,
    111, *see also* anthropology, ethnography,
    ethnology
anthropology
    applied, 83, 94–100
    and biology, 114
    and colonialism, 42, 78, 79, 82, 84–5,
    94–100
    crisis of, vii, 43, 78–9, 94–100
    and development, 78
    of difference, 2–3, 14, 82, 83, 91, 92
    histories of, vii, 1, 8, 14, 16
    and history, 1–13, 15, 78–9, 94–100,
    112–14
    and militancy, 94–100
    and modern society, 101–8
    object of, 79–90
    and objectivity, 81, 82, 94–6
    and philosophy, vii, 42–50, 82, 83
    physical, 114
Anti-Oedipus, 11, 19, 20, 28, 39, 43, 65
Augé, M., 120n.33 and 44, 121n.51
authenticity, 80–1, 92, 105, *see also*
    Lévi-Strauss, C.

Ba, H., 88
Backès-Clement, C., 40, 56–7, 59, 117 n.29
Balandier, G., 17, 35, 43, 66, 93, 116 n.1,
    117 n.19, 123 n.9
Balibar, E., 75
Bambara, the, 85
Bantu, the, 34, 84, 85
Barnes, J., 120 n.34
Barthes, R., 109
Bastian, 18
Bastide, R., 93, 94
Bataille, G., 11, 66
Baudrillard, 28, 91,
Benedict, R., 18, 37, 117 n.25
Benoist, J.-M., 109, 110,
Berreman, G. D., 78
Besançon, A., 112
bilaterality *see* kinship
Bloch, M., 119 n.17
Boas, F., 16, 28, 34
Bonté, P., 70
Bororo, the, 55, 77, 80
Bourdieu, P., 17, 45–7, 49, 54, 61, 111
Braudel, F., 112
Buijtenhuijs, R., 97

Cabral, A., 97
Camelot Project, 96–7
Cartry, M., 39
Castoriadis, C., 43, 49, 50, 76, 80, 117 n.20
Céra, the, 56–7
Certeau, M. de, 112
Césaire, A., 85
Chomsky, N., 47
clan *see* kinship
class *see* Marxism
Clastres, H,. 116 n.5
Clastres, P., 19, 91, 92, 104, 122 n.18
colonialism, 3, 42, 78, 79, 85, 90, 92, 94, 98
    106
complementary filiation *see* kinship

Index

Condominas, G., 122 n.2
contradiction *see* Marxism, myth
Conversations with Ogotomeli, 85
Corsica, 103–4
couvade, 23–4
culturalism, 3, 6, 14, 15, 17, 24, 33, 35, 39, 102, 103, 109
  and anti-culturalism, 87
  see also neo-culturalism
culture, 7, 30, 33, 34, 35, 36–41, 51, 52, 55, 76, 109

Darwin, C., 51
Deleuze, G., 15, 39, 43, 49, 65, 66, 77, 82, 91, 104, 105, 112
descent, 21, 23, 38, 39, 63, 110
determination, 65–77, 108
  and domination, 66, 67, 68, 70, 71, 75, 76, 90, 108
  see also Marxism
Devereux, G., 25
Dialectiques, 106
Dieterlen, G., 85
diffusion, 10, 18, 19, 20, 21, 22, 37,
Diola, the, 85
Dogon, the, 6–7, 29, 38, 39, 43, 85
domination *see* determination
Douglas, M., 63
dual organisation, 55
Dubois, C., 34
Dumont, L., 29–30
Durkheim, E., 7, 16, 25–33, 36, 45, 64
  and 'effervescence', 7, 31, 64
  and religion, 26–7, 31, 64
  and 'representations', 25, 26, 30, 31
  and the sacred/profane distinction, 31
  and the social fact, 26
  and the symbol/function relation, 25–33, 64
  and totemism, 27

economics, 35, 48, 58, 59, 65, *see also* Marxism
economism, 108, *see also* Marxism
'effervescence' *see* Durkheim, E.
Eggan, F., 120 n.34
Elementary Forms of the Religious Life, The, 26, 28
Elementary Structures of Kinship, The, 55
Eliade, M., 61
Elkin, A.P., 27
Engels, F., 19, 75, 89
equilibrium model, 61
Establet, R., 24
ethnocentrism, 2, 11, 12, 50, 90–4, 96
  and anti-ethnocentrism, 90–4
ethnocide, 3, 78, 91, 92, 105

ethnography, 5, 11, 25, 33, 34, 39, 41, 54, 78, 88, 91, 99
  and phantasy, 91
  and politics, 87–9
ethnology, 1, 5, 80, 82, 87–90, 93–4, 112
  and sociology, 1, 93–4
ethnophilosophy, 84, 86
ethnopsychiatry, 8, 25
Europocentrism, 91
Evans-Pritchard, E. E., 116 n.1
evolution, 10, 17, 20, 23, 26, 50, 51, 76, 100
evolutionism, 11, 12, 14, 19, 21, 22, 23, 26, 30, 38, 51, 77, 92, 95
  and 'stages', 23–4, 51
  see also 'geneticism', neo-evolutionism, 'survivals'
exaltation, state of, 27, 31, *see also* Durkheim and 'effervescence'
exchange, 55–6 57, 73, *see also* kinship
exogamy *see* kinship

feminism, 12
field-work, 37, 80, 88, 99, *see also* ethnography
folklore studies, 102–4
For Marx, 66
Fortes, M., 28, 63, 118 n.12, 120 n.34
Foucault, M., 109
Frank, A. G., 97
Freud, S., 36, 38, 39, 40, 45, 77
From Mandeville to Marx, 29
functionalism, 3, 7, 9, 10, 14, 15–17, 22–4, 29, 32–5, 38, 42–5, 49–50, 59, 61–5, 74, 75, 77, 100, 111
  and Marxism, 75, 77, 111
  and structuralism, 59, 75
  and symbolism, 61–5, 74–5, 77
Future of an Illusion, The, 38

Garanger, J., 121 nn.47 and 49
Gayton, 34
'geneticism', 54, 61, *see also* neo-evolutionism
gifts, 46, 56, *see also* exchange
Girard, R., 39
Gluckman M., 7, 17, 61, 120 nn.34 and 37
Godelier, M., 68, 69, 71, 72, 74–5, 117 n.20, 118 n.11, 120 n.44
Goldschmidt, 99
Goody, J., 118 n.12 and 13, 120 n.34
Gough, K., 78, 97, 98
Goulag *see* State
Griaule, M., 6, 37, 38, 85
Guattari, F., 39, 43, 49, 65, 77, 104, 112
Gurvitch, G., 9

126

Index

Héritier, F., 123 n.7
Herskovitz, M., 99
Heusch, L. de, 38, 117 n.27, 119 n.16, 121 n.51
L'Histoire de l'anthropologie, 17, 80
history, 5, 10–16, 18, 25, 32, 42, 51, 53, 54,
    55, 67, 78–9, 90, 92, 100, 101
    and ethnography, 90, 92
History of Ethnological Theory, The, 19, 27
Hopi, the, 34
Hountondji, P., 4, 82–4, 85, 87, 89, 92,
    122 nn.7 and 15
Hubert, H., 32
hyperstructuralism, 104

ideology, 5–6, 15, 24, 30, 31, 45, 59, 60, 65,
    74, 75, 84, 86–7, 94, 101, 104, 114
    dominant, 86–7
    'in general', 5–6, 15, 16, 24, 30, 31
    as inversion, 74
    as practice, 75, 86, 87, 94,
    and symbolism, 65, 101, 110
imperialism, 92, *see also* colonialism
incest, 38, 71, 73
    prohibition of, 55, 71, 73
incorporation *see* alliance
infrastructure, 70–2, 75, *see also* Marxism,
    superstructure
initiation *see* ritual
'instances', 35, 50, 58, 59, 65–77, 111
    and determination, 65–77
    see also 'levels'
L'Institution imaginaire de la société, 43
integration, mechanisms of, 16–18, 24, 32,
    35, 36
interdisciplinarity, 13, 111–15

Jaulin, R., 14, 19, 82, 91, 122 n.2

Kagame, Abbé, 85
Kardiner, A., 117 nn.24 and 25
kinship, 20–2, 34–5, 48, 56, 60, 67, 70, 71–3,
    89, 93, 121 nn.50–2
    and alliance, 21, 38, 59, 60, 63, 73, 89, 93
    and bilaterality, 24
    and clans, 21, 27, 30
    classificatory, 20
    cognatic, 21
    and complementary filiation, 28, 63
    Crow and Omaha systems, 20
    and domination, 70–2
    and exogamy, 56
    and infrastructure and superstructure,
      70–2, 75
    and Iroquois terminology, 23
    matrilineal, 21
    patrilineal, 20, 21, 23, 24, 26, 38, 63
Kroeber, 34

kula, 17, 35, 97
Kunyi, the, 74
Kyrn, 103

Lacan, J., 109, 110
Lacoste, Y., 123 n.28
Laplanche, J., 123 n.28
Leach, E. R. 17, 28, 35, 60, 63, 89, 118 n.12,
    119 nn.15 and 16, 120 n.33 and 34
le Goff, J., 109, 112, 123 n.13
Leroi-Gourhan, A., 66
le Roy Ladurie, E., 112, 113
'levels', 7, 17, 50, 70, *see also* 'instances'
Lévi-Strauss, C., 3, 7, 10, 16–17, 27, 33, 40,
    41, 44, 45, 48, 49, 50–60, 80, 89, 106,
    109, 110, 111, 117 n.15, 118 n.15, 120 nn.
    34 and 44, 121 nn.50 and 51
    and 'authenticity', 80–1, 84
    and field-work, 80, 106
    and kinship, 121 nn.50 and 51
    and linguistics, 111
    and myth, 48, 110
    and ritual, 48
    and totemism, 27
    and the unconscious, 7, 55–6, 81, 109
Lévy-Bruhl, L., 16
Lewis, O., 99
liminality, 62, *see also* rituals
lineage societies, 5, 46–7, 68–9
Linton, R., 24
Lombard, J., 61, 116 n.1, 120 n.34
Lowie, R., 17, 19, 21, 23, 28, 29, 34, 95,
    116 n.1
Lumumba, 4

MacGregor, 99
McNickle, 99
magic, 32, *see also* religion
Makaraziza, Monsignor, 85,
Mal de voir, Le, 87, 90
Malinowski, B., 15–17, 25, 33–6, 37, 43,
    117 n.24, *see also* functionalism
Mallarmé, S., 2, 53
Marie, A., 75
Marx, K., 19, 43, 45, 57, 66, 105, 109
Marxism, vii, 3, 5–6, 7, 9, 16, 24, 42, 43,
    49, 50, 59, 65–77, 84, 89, 105, 111
    and base and superstructure, 35, 50, 58–9,
      65–77, 111
    and class, 5, 15, 69
    and contradiction, 57, 68–9
    and economics, 16, 24, 65–6, 72, 74
    and forces of production, 68, 70, 71, 72,
      74
    and functionalism, 75, 111
    and the labour process, 68, 70
    and precapitalist societies, 15, 65–77

Index

and primitive communism, 68
and relations of production, 67, 69, 71, 74, 75
and reproduction, 71–2
and the social formation, 50, 65–77
and structural causality, 68, 74, 75
and structuralism, 66–7, 71, 75, 110–11
Mead, M., 99, 117 n.25
meaning, 6–7, 50–60, 76, 81, 99, 106
and structure, 50–60
meta-anthropology see anthropology of difference
Michelet, 113
Middleton, J., 117 n.21, 118 n.12, 120 n.34
millennialism, 4, 30, 63
Mitchell, C., 120 n.34
Moniot, H., 66, 121 n.2
Montaigne, M. de, 2
Montaillou, 112
Montesquieu, C. de, 2
Morgan, L. H., 15–16, 18, 19, 20–2, 24, 35, 88–90
and ethnology, 88–9
and 'parallelism', 21
Mulago, Abbé, 85,
Mulele, 4
Murdock, G. P., 116 n.5
myth, 29, 37–8, 40–1, 43, 44, 55–6, 61, 93, 112
and contradiction, 57
of the founding hero, 38
of incest, 38
as intellectual speculation, 59
and music, 41, 57
and mytho-logic, 46
and ritual, 59, 61, 64
Mythologies, 40, 55, 56, 59, 66

Nadel, S. F., 120 n.37
Ndembu, the 64
Needham, R., 73, 89, 118 n.12, 118 n.15, 120 n.34
négritude, 84–5
neo-culturalism, 14, 90, 91, see also culturalism
neo-evolutionism, 15, 19–20, 39, 90, 91, see also evolutionism
neo-functionalism, 49, see also functionalism
New Guinea, 17, 36
Nietzsche, F., 11, 37, 39, 62–3, 66, 109
Nkrumah, K., 85
Nora, P., 109

Oedipus complex, the 17, 29, 30, 36, 39, 112, see also anthropology of difference, psychoanalysis

Oppression et libération dans l'imaginaire, 106
Outline of a General Theory of Magic, 32
Outline of a Theory of Practice, 46

Panoff, M., 116 n.3
Paradigme perdu, Le, 30
patriarchy, 23
patrilineality, 20, 21, 23, 24, 26, 38, 63
Paysans du Languedoc, Les, 113
Perrot, C.-H., 113
Philosophie bantoue, La, 83, 85
philosophy, 37, 42–50, 82–3, 85, 87, see also anthropology
Pietrasanta, M. A. 103–4
pluri-evolutionism, 26
polyandry, 34
polygyny, 34
Pontalis, J.-B., 117 n.29
potlatch, 46
Pouillon, F., 120 n.38, 120 n.43, 121 n.56
Pouillon, J., 54–5, 67, 69, 72, 119n.16, 122n.2
practices, 47–9, 54, 58, 59, 61, 64, 75–6, 80, 86, 94–100, 110
militant, 94–100
political, 64
scientific, 94–100
symbolic, 75, 101
Preble, E., 117 nn.24 and 25
production see Marxism
psychoanalysis, 6, 8, 17, 29, 30, 36, 38, 39–40, 55, 109, 112,
and anthropology, 111–12
and the Oedipus complex, 17, 29, 30, 36, 39, 112
Punyi, the, 74,

Radcliffe-Brown, A. R., 16, 118 n.15
Rancière, J., 5, 6, 15, 16
Raw and the Cooked, The, 44
rebellion see ritual
reciprocity, 56–7
regionalism, 103–5
Reich, W., 66
Reichenbach, H., 122 n.23
Reiter, R. R., 116 n.6
religion, 7, 15, 16, 26–7, 30, 32, 45, 61, 62
economic function of, 45
as expression, 32, 45
history of, 61–2, 64
and magic, 26, 31
origin of, 30
sociology of, 7, 15, 16, 26–7
Renard pâle, Le, 85
Renoir, J., 10
representation, 25–33, 49, 60, see also Durkheim, E.

128

Index

reproduction *see* Marxism
Rethinking Symbolism, 47
Révolution structurale, La, 109
Rey, P. P., 65, 68–9, 70–1, 74
Ricoeur, P., 44
rites *see* rituals
Ritual Process; Structure and Anti-Structure, The, 61
rituals, 8–10, 39–40, 47–8, 58–9, 61–3
  efficacy of, 62, 64
  of initiation, 8, 61–2
  the logic of, 47–8
  and myth, 59, 64, 112
  of passage, 62
  of rebellion, 7
  of status elevation, 63
  of status reversal, 63
  the unity of, 63
Roheim, G., 123 n.8
Rousseau, J.-J., 2, 30
Roux, J., 120 n.39
Ruffié, J., 114
Rules of Sociological Method, The, 25

sacred, the, 26–7, 30–1, 32
sacrifice, 39
Sader, E., 90
Sahlins, M., 68, 118 n.14
Sartre, J.-P., 41, 81
Saussure, F. de, 54
Savage Mind, The, 44, 66
Schism and Continuity in Tribal Africa, 61
Sebag, L., 75,
Senghor, L., 85, 105
shamanism, 31
social contract, 30
social formation, the, 50, 65–77, *see also* Marxism
sociology, 1, 5, 7, 16, 25, 30, 79, 81, 92, 93–4
  autonomy of, 25–6
  and sociologism, 108
sorcery, 32, *see also* witchcraft
specularity, 7, 22, 50, 75
Sperber, D., 47
'stages' *see* evolutionism
Stalinism, 11
State, the, 3, 12, 13, 14, 20, 28, 31, 39, 67, 77, 92, 103–4
  and capitalism, 14
  and the Goulag, 103–5
  origin of, 20, 67, 77
  and regionalism, 103–5
Structural Anthropology, 41, 57, 66, 80, 81, 106
structural causality, 68, 74, 75
structuralism, vii, 3, 9, 14, 16, 21, 24, 29,

35, 39, 40, 42, 43, 44, 45, 49, 54, 56, 58, 60, 66–7, 71, 82, 93, 109–11
  and functionalism, 59
  and Marxism, 66–7, 71, 75, 110–11
  and the question of totality, 93
superstructure, 50, 58, *see also* base, Marxism
Surrealists, the, 2
'survivals', 23, 90, *see also* evolutionism
symbolism, 6–7, 21, 29, 30, 36–41, 43, 45, 49, 58, 65, 71, 74–6, 82, 94, 109,
  and culture, 36–41
  its efficacy, 58, 60, 64–5, 71, 75–6, 113
  and function, 61–5
  and ideology, 65, 74–5, 94
  individual, 38
  logic of, 21, 109
  universal, 49–50, 65
Systems of Consanguinity and Affinity of the Human Family, 20, 88

Tallensi, the, 33
Tardits, C., 113
Tempels, P., 83, 85
Terray, E., 16, 65, 68, 70–1, 74, 113, 120 n.39
Thomas, L.-V., 85, 122
Thonga, the, 38
Thurnwald, 28
Todas, the, 34
Tolowa-Tutuni, the, 34
torture, 10
totemism, 27, 30, 38, 44
Tristes Tropiques, 54–9
Trobriand Islands, the 15, 17, 33
Tugaré, the, 56–7
Tupinamba, the, 10, 104
Turner, V. W., 7, 49, 58, 61–5
Tylor, E., 16, 18, 22, 24, 26, 36

unconscious, the, 7, 16, 29, 55–6, 77, 81, 110
unifiliation, 28, *see also* kinship

Van Gennep, A., 62
Vidal, C., 87–8, 91–3, 99
Villa–Rojas, 95
Violence and the Sacred, 39

Wachtel, N., 114, 116 n.3
Weber, M., 45
witchcraft, 32, 46–7, 57, 63, 74–5, 113
  and 'pollution', 63
  and symbolic inversion, 74–5
Wilks, I., 119 n.15
Wittgenstein, L., 119 n.15

Zahan, D., 85, 117 n.26

Cambridge Studies in Social Anthropology

General Editor: Jack Goody

1 The Political Organisation of Unyamwezi
R. G. ABRAHAMS

2 Buddhism and the Spirit Cults in North-East Thailand*
S. J. TAMBIAH

3 Kalahari Village Politics: An African Democracy
ADAM KUPER

4 The Rope of Moka: Big-Men and Ceremonial Exchange in Mount Hagen, New Guinea*
ANDREW STRATHERN

5 The Majangir: Ecology and Society of a Southwest Ethiopian People
JACK STAUDER

6 Buddhist Monk, Buddhist Layman: A Study of Urban Monastic Organisation in Central Thailand
JANE BUNNAG

7 Contexts of Kinship: An Essay in the Family Sociology of the Gonja of Northern Ghana
ESTHER N. GOODY

8 Marriage among a Matrilineal Elite: A Family Study of Ghanaian Senior Civil Servants
CHRISTINE OPPONG

9 Elite Politics in Rural India: Political Stratification and Political Alliances in Western Maharashtra
ANTHONY T. CARTER

10 Women and Property in Morocco: Their Changing Relation to the Process of Social Stratification in the Middle Atlas
VANESSA MAHER

11 Rethinking Symbolism*
DAN SPERBER, Translated by Alice L. Morton

12 Resources and Population: A Study of the Gurungs of Nepal
ALAN MACFARLANE

13 Mediterranean Family Structures
Edited by J. G. PERISTIANY

14 Spirits of Protest: Spirit-Mediums and the Articulation of Consensus among the Zezuru of Southern Rhodesia (Zimbabwe)
PETER FRY

15 World Conqueror and World Renouncer: A Study of Buddhism and Polity in Thailand against a Historical Background*
S. J. TAMBIAH

16 Outline of a Theory of Practice*
PIERRE BOURDIEU, Translated by Richard Nice

17 Production and Reproduction: A Comparative Study of the Domestic Domain*
JACK GOODY

18 Perspectives in Marxist Anthropology*
MAURICE GODELIER, Translated by Robert Brain

* Also published as a paperback

130

Studies in social anthropology

19 The Fate of Shechem, or the Politics of Sex: Essays in the Anthropology
   of the Mediterranean
   JULIAN PITT-RIVERS
20 People of the Zongo: The Transformation of Ethnic Identities in Ghana
   ENID SCHILDKROUT
21 Casting out Anger: Religion among the Taita of Kenya
   GRACE HARRIS
22 Rituals of the Kandyan State
   H. L. SENEVIRATNE
23 Australian Kin Classification
   HAROLD W. SCHEFFLER
24 The Palm and the Pleiades: Initiation and Cosmology in Northwest Amazonia
   STEPHEN HUGH-JONES
25 Nomads of South Siberia: The Pastoral Economies of Tuva
   S. I. VAINSHTEIN
26 From the Milk River: Spatial and temporal processes in Northwest Amazonia
   CHRISTINE HUGH-JONES
27 Day of Shining Red: An Essay on Understanding Ritual
   GILBERT LEWIS
28 Hunters, Pastoralists and Ranchers: Reindeer Economies and their Transformations
   TIM INGOLD
29 The Wood-carvers of Hong Kong: Craft Production in the World Capitalist
   Periphery
   EUGENE COOPER
30 Minangkabau Social Formations: Indonesian Peasants and the World Economy
   JOEL S. KAHN
31 Patrons and Partisans: A Study of Two Southern Italian *Comuni*
   CAROLINE WHITE
32 Muslim Society
   ERNEST GELLNER
33 Why Marry Her? Society and Symbolic Structures
   LUC DE HEUSCH
34 Chinese Ritual and Politics
   EMILY MARTIN AHERN
35 Parenthood and Social Reproduction: Fostering and Occupational Roles in
   West Africa
   ESTHER N. GOODY
36 Dravidian Kinship
   THOMAS R. TRAUTMANN

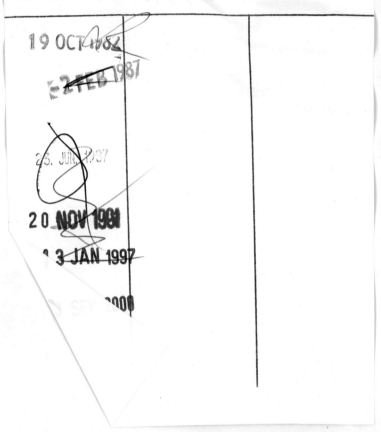